Game Shooting

Best Wishes

John King

JOHN KING

ISBN 978-0-9926292-0-5

Published by John King in conjunction with Acorn Independent Press

Published by
www.johnkingcoaching.com
admin@johnkingcoaching.com
www.acornindependentpress.com

I would like to dedicate this book to all the shoot owners
and their families who have given me such fabulous
sport and so generously treated me to the warmest of
hospitality over many years.

Also, a very special thank you to them; their gamekeepers and
hard working teams, for always going that ‘extra mile’
to ensure that every game day was a memorable
occasion for my visiting client Guns.

I am so privileged to have been on all these wonderful shoots.

Titles By John King

Books & eBooks

Clay Shooting For Beginners and Enthusiasts (Print edition ISBN 9780956346117)
Clay Shooting For Beginners and Enthusiasts (Kindle edition 9780956346131)
Clay Shooting For Beginners and Enthusiasts (iBooks edition ISBN 9780956346155)
Game Shooting (Print edition ISBN 9780992629205)
Game Shooting (Kindle edition ISBN 9780992629212)
Game Shooting (iBooks edition 9780992629229)

DVDs

Clay Shooting From Scratch DVD (ISBN 9780956346124)
Sporting Clays Shooting From Scratch NTSC version For USA TV systems
(ISBN 9780956346186)

John King's eBooks can be purchased from Amazon's Kindle Store and Apple's iBookstore. In the United Kingdom Books and DVDs can be purchased form all the major book retailers, or previewed and purchased at:

www.johnkingcoaching.com

Acknowledgements

So many people have helped me with putting this book together; that I am nervous that I should leave some worthy contributor out:

In an attempt to prevent any careless omissions, I am playing for safe and putting people in the categories that they helped me with.

The order of listing should not in any way be misinterpreted as any order of priority or importance. Everyone's contribution has been very important to me.

Photography: (By far the longest list); Don Brunt from his Double Barrelled Picture Companies extensive library, Richard (Buzz) Round-Turner, Allan, Ashley & Hayley Giles, David White, Cindy & Tony of Wiltshire Rod & Gun, Swindon, GMK Ltd, Boss & Co Best London Gunmakers, Alan Paine Country Clothing, Will Hetherington at Shooting Gazette, Roddey & Jane Dowd, Calum Forsyth, Paul Gerrard, Peter Thompson GWCT, Andrew King.

Behind The Scenes: A special mention to Allan Giles, who has been Gamekeeping for so long, he can't remember! His generous and selfless input has been invaluable in helping me put the Behind The Scenes chapter together.

Computing: Terry & Andrew King who regularly covered for their 'Old Man's' computing/word processing inadequacies.

Recipes: Jo; for her mouth-watering recipes. Yes they taste as good as they read.

Copy Editing, Typesetting & Proofreading: A special thank you to Ali and Leila at Acorn Independent Press for their patient, persistent professionalism.

Finally, but definitely neither last nor least, much deserved recognition to Maureen, my long-suffering Wife, for her tolerance as deadline dates drew closer!

Contents

Foreword

Quite a few decades ago, I was a new boy to shooting and learned the hard way - I wish I had a book like this; every page is packed full of valuable lessons for anyone from novice to expert. John covers the essential parts of the sport providing an insight into all aspects of the activity from the behind-the-scenes work of the game keeper and his team to the logisitics of organising shooting days and even offers advice on the social side of the sport. This is a book that I will open before every season starts and every day's shooting I have the privilege to attend or host.

The coaching chapters of this book are very easy to follow and understand, and are given clarity by very professional diagrams. Personally, I particularly value the chapter on shooting high pheasant and hope that my 'next day' produces a better yield than my last.

John has been bringing shooting parties to Eddington in Berkshire for around fifteen years; although some of the party often comprise inexperienced shots, they always behave and shoot with the prowess and the sporting outlook that I associate with John and his dedication to preparing his pupils for the traditional sport of game shooting.

I commend this concise instruction manual to you as the ideal companion on the journey to your next shooting day.

Sir Peter Michael

Introduction to Game Shooting

By way of introduction, I would like to explain what this book is about and how it is set out.

My objective is to describe a logical sequence of events and the learning processes that mirror the typical programmes undergone by the huge numbers of pupils that I have coached in preparation for game shooting.

It was recently calculated (very scarily) that I had coached in excess of 30,000 pupils over the past 25 years including many pupils who have returned for numerous lessons. I would estimate that around 70% of those 30,000 pupil sessions have involved me coaching and preparing people for some form of British game shooting. Whilst I enjoy all my coaching sessions; game shooting has always given me the greatest satisfaction.

The majority of game shooting pupils fit into three broad categories: **Young Shots**. Almost always youngsters growing up within game shooting families; often living on land that has a game shoot or being related to game shoot owners. These young folk are a joy to teach and spend time with. Generally they arrive for their first coaching session at around 11 years of age, but there have been a few starting as young as 8 years old.

That might seem very young but I promise you that they are ready. They are all very keen and do bear in mind that they have been out in the field getting involved in all aspects of game shooting from the age of 3 or 4. Part of growing

(Left) The author's grandson, Alfie, aged 10 . First Day! First birds! (Right) Another happy Young Shot with his first bird! First day!

up in a gun-owning family means that they have been indoctrinated about safety from a very early age. They will also have spent time with the gamekeeper and will definitely have worked regularly in the beating line, which ensures that they understand and respect the huge amount of background work that goes on to produce a successful game shoot.

Over the years, it has been my great privilege to stand with so many of these Young Shots when they participate in their first game day on the family shoot. The cheers reverberate for miles when they bring down their first bird (to their constant embarrassment my cheer is generally the loudest!) The greatest pleasure is, of course, that these youngsters enjoy these successes in the company and full view of their families - there will often be three generations in attendance.

Although these young folk become very safe competent shots at a very early age, they are supervised closely by an adult until they are much older.

Happy young lady game shots enjoying their day

The second category of game shooting pupil is the **Experienced Shot**. He/she (yes the girls shoot too! And do so very well) probably started like the youngsters that I have just been describing, and may well be people that I taught from scratch when they were young.

They are invariably good shots, but because they only shoot for a few months of the year; they get out of practice and like to sharpen up. Also everyone who shoots can get a little apprehensive about performing below par amongst their peers.

These Experienced Shots will also appear at the shooting school if they feel that they did not shoot up to their own previous standard on their last day out, and they will definitely appear if they receive a particularly important shooting invitation. For example, I may get a young man saying something like 'I am shooting with my Father-in-law, he always watches me like a hawk'.

With these first two categories of pupils my focus is on shooting systems and technique. My role is simply to unlock their potential to shoot well because they already know about safety, shooting etiquette, good sportsmanship, dress codes and everything else in the game shooting scene.

There is a third category of game shooting pupil that I have spent countless pleasurable hours with: **The Novice Game Shot**. This person arrives with me for the first shooting lesson and says 'I want to be a game shot'. When they tell me that they want to be game shots my retort is 'Fantastic' but if you want to learn game shooting with me, please start with the full acceptance that a game day is a traditional rural social occasion with some rules and a set of etiquette and if you are lucky, some shooting!' Working with these pupils is the most interesting thing that I do because they are about to enter a world that they know nothing or very little about. I have discovered that when these people realize how much there is to learn, they apply themselves wholeheartedly to learning as much as they can about their new pastime. Their pleasures in their own new successes are immensely rewarding for me.

My hope is that the remainder of this book mirrors the programmes that these newcomers to game shooting follow and provides you with the same information and pleasures that they enjoy whilst learning.

When the newcomer arrives for the first game shooting lesson (Chapter Four), I need to ensure that he (for simplicity and continuity sake, we have already established that the pupil could be of either gender) has a clear understanding of what a formal driven game day entails. My experience has shown me that newcomers conjure up widely different ideas about what a game day is; so Chapter One will give a full description of a typical formal driven game day. Dispelling the first myth that 'formal' does not mean 'stuffy'. It simply means that there is a complete organization around the day.

The pupil quickly realizes that game shooting has its own jargon and terminology so the more common terms are explained in Chapter One and throughout the book.

The actual reality of the newcomer's learning programme and progress is that information is passed on piecemeal, conversationally and informally during hour long lessons (commonly around six) taken over a period of weeks and months.
In order to ensure that this book passes on the same information that is given to all

the newcomers, a structured presentation is my only option. Therefore Chapter Two will describe the different types of game shooting taking place in Britain today, including the species of game birds in the chronological order of their seasons.

The pupils that experience this process of learning and introduction to a new sport and pastime tend to share certain traits: Economics; game shooting is a relatively expensive activity to become involved in; so the adult new comer is usually of a certain age (35+) and is either a successful business person or professional. They are all without exception 'achievers' and as such have very high expectations of themselves; their desire to learn and succeed is very high, which is very positive (although it can lead to periods of great frustration for them) because they soak up as much information as I can give them. They are naturally curious about the history of game shooting in Britain; therefore Chapter Three is set aside to provide a very basic historical background.

Most of these newcomers will have done some clay shooting, possibly on corporate days or during stag events; so they will have a good understanding of safe gun handling. Chapter Four describes the first game shooting lesson with me, including the safety aspects of field shooting and the best shooting system to master targets (from now on called birds) driven towards us and incoming crossing right to left. The system that is explained during this chapter is called '**The Method**', and during this lesson, the pupil is also shown how to apply The Method to pairs of birds shooting a right-and-left and where this term comes from. By the end of this lesson, gun mounting, shooting driven pairs and crossing pairs has been fully explained. This chapter also highlights the problems and solutions associated with dominant eyes.

During Chapter Five the lessons go on to demonstrate how to cope with various angled birds as they appear unexpectedly and learning the correct footwork to deal with them. The pupil is taught how to react to multiple birds in preparation for shooting partridges flying in coveys. Also included in this training for partridge shooting, is the systematic sequence of turning around to take a safe shot at a partridge flying straight away behind.

Taking a break between shooting lessons, I have used Chapter Six to describe guns, cartridges, game shooting clothing, accessories and associated equipment because this represents quite a large part of the newcomer's learning programme. The equipment described in this chapter also encompasses advice about obtaining a shotgun certificate and Public Liability insurance

The focus in Chapter Seven is very much on the coaching required to develop the pupil's skills to overcome the challenges presented by high flying pheasant.

Before any newcomer pupil is taken out to participate on a game day; the lessons will include an introduction to the actual physical reality of shooting with **neighbours** (other people with guns spaced about 30yds to either side). This is of course necessary to heighten the awareness of all the safety parameters required and to teach the newcomers the rules of etiquette.

Every pupil has to understand safe, sporting, sociable shooting, which means only taking a shot when it is safe to do so, only taking a bird that is **sporting** (one that is high enough and far enough away to present a challenge) and most importantly, understanding which birds are his and which are his neighbour's. The safety, good sportsmanship and etiquette rules described in detail in this chapter are essential as they represent the last lesson prior to the newcomer's first experience on a formal driven game day.

While the pupil gets a break from the pressures of learning at the shooting school, he is taken (and I would like you to come along too) to get a behind-the-scenes look at some of the equipment used and gain an understanding of the huge amount of input and hard work required to produce successful game shooting.

Chapter Eight will be dedicated to demonstrating the strategic siting of **release pens** (the protective enclosures designed to keep the poults safe from predators whilst they are reared to maturity) and siting of **cover crops and game strips** (areas of maize, kale, artichokes, mustard and other suitable plants that provide sheltered feeding and avenues of movement for the birds and strategic places for the birds to fly from). This chapter will also provide a basic chronological description of the gamekeeper's year to reinforce just how much planning, effort and expense is required to produce the best game shooting

The penultimate chapter (Chapter Nine) will describe a typical first formal driven day starting with the **shoot captain's brief** and drawing numbers, establishing safety parameters at the first peg, marking birds down and liaising with the picking-up team and recognizing the crucial work and skills of the dogs and their handlers. It will also describe elevenses, lunch, tea and the social aspects of a shoot day. I will be describing the all-important blanking-in efforts of the beaters whilst the Guns are lunching, which ensures the success of the final big drive, the end of day, tipping the keeper and accepting a brace of birds. The brace of birds taken at the end of the day are, of course, taken home to be cooked and the remainder of the birds shot during that day are hung in the cool room to await collection by the game dealer. It is his responsibility to ensure that they are correctly prepared for entering the food distribution chain; via supply to hotels, restaurants and supermarkets.

Game bird meat is becoming increasingly popular so the final chapter (Chapter Ten) will offer you some mouth-watering recipes. Lest you think that I have suddenly developed super new culinary skills (no, I am staying firmly on the eating side!), it is our expert Chef who has so generously and skilfully provided a selection of her superb partridge and pheasant recipes in the final chapter.

Before We Start

I have been having tremendous fun since I first became involved in shooting field sports at the age of eight: With catapult, bow and arrow (all home-made of course) air rifle and finally shotgun; I have enjoyed countless hours of fun in the field.

During the past 25 years I have enjoyed yet even more fun being allowed to pass on the pleasures and joys of game shooting to newcomers. I am now going to have tremendous fun preparing this book and would like you to join me in the hope that you have fun too!

Notes on Quantitative Descriptions

During ensuing chapters I may need to offer quantitative descriptions to best portray various aspects of game shooting. Aside from the bulging pages of the game books of the Edwardian 'Great Shoots' proudly listing their huge 'bags' and extolling the shooting feats of the famous guests; there is a great scarcity of accurate figures describing our sport.

Thankfully the Countryside Alliance has come to my rescue and has kindly provided me with a copy of the SHOOTING FACTS report published August 2006: The British Association for Shooting and Conservation, The Country Land and Business Association, The Countryside Alliance in conjunction with the Game Conservancy Trust; joined together to commission Public and Corporate Economic Consultants (PACEC) to provide an independent assessment of the economic and environmental contribution of shooting to the UK. A copy of the full report is available at www.shootingfacts.co.uk. PACEC conducted their extensive research throughout 2004. Below is a precis of their main findings:

- 480,000 people shoot live quarry.
- Shooting supports the equivalent of 70,000 full time jobs.
- Shooters spend £2 billion each year on goods and services.
- Shooting is worth £1.6 billion to the UK economy.
- Shooting is involved in the management of two-thirds of the rural land area of the UK. Two million hectares are actively managed for conservation as a result of shooting.
- Shoot providers spend £250 million a year on conservation.
- Shooters spend 2.7 million work days on conservation - the equivalent of 12,000 full time jobs.

Any descriptive figures that I use throughout the following pages, are solely my own estimates based on and/or extrapolated from this *Shooting Facts* report; combined with my own experiences and observations: Resultant errors or misrepresentations are totally my own responsibility.

Chapter One
A Formal Driven Game Day

A traditional rural group activity that takes place at a venue which has the facilities to produce sufficient quantities of game birds that can be encouraged to fly in a sporting manner over a **team** (normally 8, could be 6, 7 or up to 10) of game shooting participants; the **Guns** (throughout the remainder of this book 'Guns' describe people using shotguns in the legitimate pursuit of game birds). The meeting venue of the game shoot, may be a country house on a large estate, it might be a farmhouse that has a game shoot on the farm land. It could also be an hotel or pub adjacent to the estate or farm.

On a large estate that hosts many game days every game season the Guns may meet up at a building built or converted specifically for hosting visiting teams of shooting parties called a **shooting lodge**. This could be a very grand affair providing en-suite accommodation for the Guns and their partners. Conversely it could be a small, humble shelter such as an old barn or stable. The shoot lodge facilities will match the status of the shoot.

The team of Guns will be met by the **shoot host** (also sometimes known as the shoot captain). A host is generally the owner of the actual game shoot. A shoot captain is generally a senior employee of the owner or an appropriate person specifically designated to carry out that role on a shoot day. **The host** and **captain** fulfill the same roles in that they are there to look after the Guns, to be the liaison between the Guns and the game keeping team and generally be responsible for the safe and smooth running of the day. It is increasingly common that some of our biggest

Guns being welcomed and briefed by the shoot host at the country estate house

game shoots are owned by absent owners residing abroad; in these circumstances, the **estate manager** is often the designated shoot captain.

Most teams of Guns are expected to arrive at around 9 a.m. unless the day is planned to start with a sit down breakfast (as my days do) when the day will start at around 8.30 a.m.

The host will make every one welcome and brief the Guns about the days programme, proceedings and special rules.

He will allocate people into 4 wheel drive (4WD) vehicles, or in some cases will instruct the Guns to place all of their necessary shooting equipment into one special vehicle that will transport the whole team around the shoot. This could be a converted or custom built trailer towed by a tractor; it could also be a large 4WD ex-military vehicle converted to carry up to around 20 people (to make room for non-shooting spectating guests). Regardless of the type and make up of this single mode of transport that will carry all the Guns; it will be known as the **Gun bus**. Gun Buses could be compared to shoot lodges in terms of status and comfort - they can be very luxurious or extremely cold and uncomfortable. Their purpose is to encourage closer social interaction between Guns that may not know each other and maintain the best social ambiance which they certainly do. Also having the Guns all together makes life easier for the host to ensure that all of his Guns are always at the right place at the right time.

The host will tell the Guns which species may be shot on the day, the signals which indicate when shooting may commence and when it must cease on each drive that they should listen out for. He will lay out the programme for the day, telling the Guns about lunch and tea arrangements including the likely time of departure; usually around 4.30 p.m. Finally, he will explain the numbering system and the number of **drives** that are likely to take place during the day.

A drive is both a named location somewhere on the shoot and a period of time taken for a team of **beaters** to move through an area of land which will invariably be a combination of woodland and cover crops (also called game strips). The team of beaters is controlled by a single gamekeeper or gamekeepers. The **beaters** are a group of people (usually between 10-20) which carry sticks or flags. Their role is to walk slowly and steadily towards the line of Guns through cover crops and/or woodland tapping their sticks and shaking their flags. The objective being to encourage the partridges/pheasants to walk, then eventually **flush** (take off and fly) towards and then over the Guns at a sporting height.

The Guns will have been spaced out along a line of numbered pegs set around 30 yards apart. These sets of pegs will be situated strategically around the shoot; each set marking the location of a named drive. The pegs take a variety of forms, ranging from hedgerow sticks, smart white painted stakes and logs through to sturdy boxes custom-made to hold empty cartridge cases. What they all have in common is a clearly marked number; on an eight Gun shoot the numbers will be 1 to 8.

The Beaters. The 'engine' of every game shoot. 'First drive over, off to the next one'.

Peg drawing systems, game book and dog whistle.

The Host will have taken the assembled Guns through a simple random draw of numbers; probably by inviting each Gun to select a small metal peg from a small leather wallet. The pegs are face down in the wallet so that the Gun does not know what actual number he is selecting. When all 8 pegs have been drawn from the wallet each Gun will know which numbered peg he must stand on for the first drive. The host will have explained how many numbers each Gun should move between each drive.

If his brief was 'move up three', then each Gun knows that he must stand on a peg three numbers higher than he did on the previous drive. So Gun number 1 on the first drive, will stand on peg number 4 on the second drive, and peg number 7 on the third drive and so on. This is a rudimentary attempt to try to spread out the amount of shooting each Gun enjoys fairly, because as a rough rule of thumb, the greatest amount of birds tend to fly over the middle numbers.

(Left) A line of (lady) Guns on their pegs on a cold frosty morning. (Right) A typical game peg, this one sturdy enough to support the weight of this heavy leather cartridge bag.

The hard working beating team and their dogs in the beaters' wagon, en-route to the next drive

Upon the completion of each drive, the beaters embark into their transport to travel to a beating start point of the next one. Their transport will be similar to the Gun bus but probably more basic and generally known as the **Beaters' wagon.**

A typical driven day would include 3-4 drives during the morning and one big drive after lunch. Drives commonly last from 20 to 40 minutes; an after lunch drive could last from 50 minutes to 1 hour.

In addition to a team of Guns and a team of beaters; most established shoots would have a picking-up team of at least three people. These **Pickers-Up** (yes that is what we really call them!) go behind the Guns with their trained dogs to pick up the fallen birds, and most importantly, to quickly retrieve wounded birds to ensure that they are humanely dispatched. It is common for a picker-up to be seen working 3 dogs, but the number can be as high as 5 or 6. The picking-up teams tend to move around the shoot in their own 4WD vehicles which they need to house their dogs. Larger shoots need bigger picking-up teams. I watched a team of 12 working a few weeks ago.

A big part of the shoot host's role is to ensure that the social aspects of the day are successful. This starts with a warm welcome as the Guns arrive, followed by his informative brief which tells the Guns exactly what is going to happen, what the rules are, and ensures everybody relaxes and gets to know each other.

The next important social event in the day's programme will be elevenses (usually, after a couple of drives). The host will gather the Guns (and their non-shooting guests) together in a comfortable spot (shade on a hot late September partridge day or the warmth and shelter of a barn on a wet or bitterly cold January day). There will be plenty of cool drinks on the warmer days and piping hot soup on the colder ones. Simple snacks accompany the drinks and soup, with hot sausages topping the popularity polls. Tradition dictates that a small tot of sloe gin follows the snacks. This is often home made by the host family/team.

The host tries to maintain a relaxed atmosphere as he ushers the Guns around between the drives, but he does have a timed programme to adhere to. He will almost certainly be in radio contact with the gamekeeper/(s) and mobile telephone contact with the kitchen of the shoot house/lodge/hotel/pub, because lunch is the next important social aspect of the day.

Shoot lunches are generally of a generous hours duration giving the Guns ample time to socialise with each other; often they have met for the first time that day. Many lasting friendships are made on game days, as are very many mutually fruitful business associations. Lunch could be a speedier affair. However whilst the Guns are relaxing, the keepers and their beating teams are

Beaters working through a maize crop

carrying out an extremely important task: They are **blanking-in** which means that these beating teams are covering quite large areas (often working for 30/40 minutes) gently moving forward tapping their sticks to move the game birds to strategic areas of cover, so that when the Guns arrive on their pegs, there is very little time to wait before the birds begin to flush over the Guns. These 'After Lunch' big drives can be very exciting and testing; the adrenalin rushes ensure that this is the most memorable part of the day.

Tea is the next event, and almost always includes generous slices of home-made cakes. Further sustenance is not actually required by the Guns, however this period of time is very important to the keeper and his team. His pickers-up have to ensure that all the birds from the last drive have been gathered up, **Braced up** (tied together in pairs) and finally counted.

Now the head-keeper joins up with the shoot host, firstly to advise him of the total **bag** for the day (numbers of birds by species shot during the day) i.e. how many pheasants and partridges, also how many 'various' (non-game species: crow, pigeon, magpie, jay) have been shot. Many of the Guns like to enter these details in their **game books** (records of each day that they shoot on, including the names of the other Guns). Many shoots provide each Gun with a game card to take away. This card has the name of the shoot, date of the event, names of the Guns and the breakdown of the bag.

Some teams of Guns also like to enter a 'sweep' whereby every Gun makes a guess as to the bag and pays an agreed sweep levy. The Gun with the most accurate guess wins the sweep pot. The sweep winner often awards his winnings wholly or partially to a nominated charity. The final social ritual of the day sees the Guns being given a **brace** (two) of game birds by the keeper; they in turn tip him as a reinforcement of their verbal thanks for his efforts during the day. Most Guns will seek the advice of the shoot host as to an appropriate amount to tip.

(Left) One man and his six dogs. The Picker-Up, essential on any game day.
(Right) The Guns at lunch in the shoot lodge.

"Bracing the birds". Tying them in pairs to hang them on the rails of the game cart to allow air to flow around them; keeping them fresh until they can be hung in the game 'cool room'.

After the Guns have departed, the host and keeper will discuss the day (probably accompanied by a well-earned glass of something pleasant) in preparation for the next shoot. Each of the Guns (if they were invited guests) have their thank you letter to pen to the host as they ponder the high birds that beat them.

Now you have a clear idea of the make-up of a formal driven game day from start to finish and, at risk of stating the obvious, the beaters' efforts are primarily to encourage the game birds to fly towards and over the line of Guns. There is however quite a variance in the styles and levels of driven game shooting over a very broad spectrum:

Types of Shoots

At one end of the spectrum is the large private estate that runs a programme not dissimilar to the one that I have described. These are in decline as the shooting is provided solely for the private use of the families and their very privileged guests; so therefore it is extremely costly to finance.

At the opposite end of the game shooting spectrum, is an operation that is totally self-help and almost always run on a shoe-string. We would be looking at a group of friends (probably between 10-20) that have developed a small shoot totally by their own efforts. Typically they will have secured the use of a small area of land, maybe up to a few hundred acres via an informal lease whereby the land owner/s are given their shooting F.O.C (free of charge), in return for the areas set aside for cover crops, plus machinery and labour to plant and maintain these areas. Arable land owners may also contribute the wheat aspects of the game bird feed. The remainder of the group will club together to provide the essential finances for the cost of the gamebird poults and any necessary equipment and social costs. By the very nature of these rural activities; most successful self-help groups will have recruited the local country pub landlord into their ranks, thereby ensuring the regular supply of all necessary sustenance and shelter! The remainder of the group will allocate their varying skills and lifestyles to produce the most efficient operation. The bulk of the gamekeeping tasks (including vermin control) are carried out by retired countrymen with appropriate skills (especially lucky groups may include a retired game keeper). Artisans in the group can carry out the practical construction work; pen building/ repair etc.

On an actual shoot day, everyone will need to make their physical contribution because, almost certainly, the day will be run on a **walk-and-stand** basis (a number of the group will line out on pegs, whilst the others will become the beaters and the essential picking-up team). On completion of each drive, roles are reversed; beaters become Guns and Guns become beaters. This self-help style of shooting is the most economical and a fantastically enjoyable way to be involved in all aspects of game shooting. However, human nature being what it is, the rare long-term success of these groups is only achieved when all members continue to make an equal contribution and everyone involved focuses on the same objectives.

Next up the ladder is the **syndicate** – a group made up of 'Full' and 'Half Guns'. As implied by the titles, the Full Guns have paid an amount that allows them to shoot on every syndicate day, (commonly 8-10 days) and, obviously, the Half Guns only attend half of these days. Syndicates can be very low key; arrangements are made with a farmer (or farmers) who operate shooting on a self-help basis, although they may employ a part-time gamekeeper. These farmers sell a certain number of days to the syndicate, and quite often part of the syndicate fees are offset by providing a certain amount of shooting to the farmer/s.

Syndicates do also operate much higher up the financial scale with higher fees, some private estates agree to let a certain number of days at an agreed **bag size** (a reasonable number of birds that could be expected to be shot during the day by a competent team of Guns). Part of the agreement about the bag expectation would include discussion and agreement about the degree of difficulty and challenge provided by the birds on the shoot. A shoot considered as a '1 in 4' venue, would need to present on average 400 sporting birds over a team of 8 Guns to produce an expected bag of 100 birds. For an expected bag of 200 birds, the estate would aim to present 800 sporting birds over the Guns.

Another type of syndicate is the **roving syndicate**; generally a couple of financial notches above the static syndicate. This is where a group of like-minded Guns get together and agree to take a certain number of days at agreed bag sizes; but they like to travel around to experience a variety of shooting at different venues. One of the most experienced members of the group will be nominated as the organizer, it will be his responsibility to book suitable venues and collect everyone's shooting fees. He may book directly with individual shoots, or he may seek out the services of a **sporting agency** (a business that has the sole function of selling and organizing field sports activities; often on a global basis. That might be pheasant shooting in Devon, partridge shooting in Spain or salmon fishing in Norway). The sporting agent will charge a fee, adding to the roving syndicates costs, but taking away all the organisational responsibilities.

An increasing number of private shoots now let some days to cater for the growing number of roving syndicates and the demand from the sporting agents. This is a very effective way of offsetting the substantial costs of maintaining a quality game shoot. Typically, these shoots will retain two or three days for their own private use, maybe also host 8 to 10 days for a local static syndicate, and in addition let a few other days to people they know well or possibly to a sporting agent.

There is one other popular type of British driven game shoot: I have left this one until last, but it is by no means least! I am showing my own bias, because it is very much my own preferred type the **farm shoot**, the bedrock of game shooting! This is almost always self-keepered now, that means the farming family, possibly farm staff and maybe a retired keeper; carry out all keepering work. The beaters will be retired farm-workers, family and friends, children and a few other volunteers (some will be paid). The picking-up team will be from within a close network of friends and everyone's social needs will be met in the farmhouse or, occasionally, the local village pub. The Guns will be neighbouring farmers and others involved in the agricultural world.

These farm days generally start a little later than others and almost always have the shoot lunch at the end of the day. This is because traditionally those involved with running the shoot had/have other important daily tasks to perform related to livestock; before and after the shoot.

I do not describe this type of shoot as the 'bedrock' casually. During the school holidays, most of these farm shoots will have at least one youngster in the line. Very often the whole line of Guns will be Young Shots; all closely supervised by volunteer experienced Guns who happily give up their time to ensure that many more responsible Young Shots are introduced to this wonderful traditional rural pursuit. They are the future!

I myself, have been very privileged to be invited to help introduce these young people to game shooting; it always gives me a great thrill to do it, and long may that continue. The vast majority of adult newcomers to game shooting that I coach have their first season's experiences on mixed pheasant/partridge shoots and those will probably be on the private shoots that let a few days; which is where I mainly take my teams of Guns. There are, however, other game bird species, each with their own season; which will be explained in the next chapter.

Chapter Two
The Most Common Species of British Game Birds

Although, the vast majority of newcomers that I help to prepare for game shooting will be participating in partridge or pheasant shooting, a small minority will have their first shooting experience in the game field in a grouse butt; due to geographic location or family/friends/connections. For this small group, I am never sure whether I should be green with envy or pessimistic about their chances of success! (But more about this later).

Most of our casual chatter during the game shooting coaching sessions will be based around the forthcoming partridge and pheasant shooting that the pupil is going to be participating in; which also happens to be the sphere where I have had the most experience. However, other forms of game shooting will, invariably, be mentioned and it seems only logical that this chapter lists the most common bird species in the British game shooting calendar alongside the dates of the seasons within which they can be legally shot.

At this juncture I am acutely aware that some of the bird species mentioned in this chapter will receive only short coverage. The reason for this is firstly; that most of my pupils are unlikely to encounter these species (certainly in their early years of game shooting) and secondly, whilst I have experienced most forms of game shooting, there are certainly areas where I feel that my experiences are insufficient to qualify me to write about them at length. I would like to stress to those of you who are avid and passionate followers of species that I only give scant coverage to please accept that I am not in any way being dismissive of your chosen preference.

A chronological order of dates and seasons appears to present the simplest approach:

Types of Game Birds and Seasons

12th August to 31st January - The Common Snipe

Although there is nothing common about its style of flight as it bursts from under your feet out of a black and clinging Irish bog! Well there is the main clue; most organized snipe shooting parties head across the water to Ireland (surely that lovely silk smooth Guinness cannot also be an attraction!). Common snipe are of course found and shot in other areas that have permanent bog or wetland, particularly in the far South West. They will also fleetingly visit flooded areas.

From time to time, I am confronted with 'can you give me a lesson for snipe shooting please, a group of us are off to Ireland next week ?'. This always causes me some head-scratching, as I have yet to come across a clay trap that will launch its target into the air like a rocket, whilst it jinks (swerves) unexpectedly at every conceivable angle. However, I suspect my failings as the snipe coach have never prevented the pupil from enjoying his most exciting shooting (and yes one of his very expensive shooting boots still sits at the bottom of an Irish bog!).

12th August to 10th December - The Grouse

Subjective statement now: 'To be stood in a grouse butt and have a **covey** (a group of 3 or more grouse, commonly consisting of 8-12 birds) of wild grouse suddenly appear 80 yards in front skimming towards the butt, a few feet above the heather, each one jinking and swerving like a fighter plane is, in my opinion, the most challenging and exciting of all forms of game bird shooting!'

The grouse butt is a man-made structure, it could be stone, but is commonly made of peat blocks. Its purpose is to provide partial concealment of the Gun in what is often very open moorland. These butts are numbered just the same as pegs

Unlike the majority of partridges and pheasants that we shoot; the grouse is a truly wild bird, with truly wild survival instincts. If the Guns stood tall and proud against the sky line, the grouse would almost surely jink away and never fly over the butts.

Native Red Grouse

Grouse over the butts the most exhilarating game shooting experience as the grouse jink and swerve across heather, imitating a squadron of low-flying fighter airplanes

Probably in direct proportion to the excitement of shooting grouse, is the effort, expertise and cost of producing a successful driven grouse shooting day. Grouse shoots, more correctly described as **grouse moors** are found in Scotland and parts of the North of England. As the grouse moor title implies, these geographic areas have the natural heather moorland habitat which is essential for the survival of this game bird species.

In comparison to the average partridge/pheasant shoots, grouse moors tend to be much larger scale and require intense husbandry to maintain the habitat. A big part of that husbandry is carefully timed and monitored heather burning to ensure that there are sufficient quantities of healthy heather at just the right stage of growth at the critical period of grouse breeding. When the grouse chicks hatch there needs to be sufficient cover so that the young birds can be kept dry and warm. There also needs to be enough insect life to ensure an appropriate food supply. Alongside the husbandry of these vast areas is the need for the game keepers to keep a constant control of the vermin.

It is very rare for any grouse moor to achieve many uninterrupted years of success. Wet and cold weather during the critical breeding period can result in the cancellation of a whole season's shooting. Grouse are also susceptible to diseases which are difficult to control over such large areas.

The organisational and social aspects of the driven grouse day are similar to a driven partridge/pheasant day, although the Guns will almost always be met and hosted at a shoot lodge; and, due to the difficult terrain, may well need to be transported around the moor in specially adapted tracked vehicles. They are also likely to lunch alfresco on the moor due to the greater distances travelled.

The grouse beating team is likely to be bigger on a moor as great areas of heather need to be covered, requiring high levels of fitness and stamina. Walking miles through thick heather makes walking across plough or grassland pale into insignificance. The picking-up dogs may well be in the beating line as the moorland terrain often dictates that it is unsafe to have people behind the line of butts.

Each grouse moor has a signal that the host will have explained to the Guns during his brief. This signal (probably some form of horn), will be loud and distinguishable. The Guns will have been told that they will hear the signal when the beating line is within about 300 yards of the line of butts. Their brief will have been that no further shooting towards the beaters is to take place (because the birds often fly just a few feet above the heather, so all the grouse passing over or between the butts may only be shot safely behind. This of course precludes anyone being behind the line because the Guns could otherwise shoot directly towards the beaters.)

The bag size of a grouse day is always described as a number of brace so that a day that resulted in 102 grouse being shot, would be described as a 51 brace day. That is a very respectable bag for modern grouse shooting.

Driven grouse is by far the most expensive type of game shooting, due to the extraordinary costs involved. However it is possible to experience grouse shooting much less expensively if you are prepared to be a Gun on a walked-up day. Not for the unfit or faint-hearted, because as the title implies, the Guns walk through the heather and must cover huge distances. Fantastic fun in magnificent scenery (as all grouse shooting is - mist and fog allowing!). Every bird shot is well earned and adds to a bag that is usually quite small, totalling just a few brace. The walking is generally done with dogs flushing out the birds, with the most luxurious being done over Pointers. These dogs actually stop 'on point' so that the Guns know where the birds are going to flush from and can be ready to shoot.

During July and early August I know I am going to be giving lessons to prepare my pupils for grouse shooting. I thoroughly enjoy these sessions but I always find myself feeling slightly envious: I can picture the sort of topography and scenery that these people are going to be shooting in, and can almost feel the adrenalin rush that they are going to feel when those grouse come hurtling over the butts!

1st September to 31st January - The Duck

A large variety of ducks are included on the game list, but by far the most common inland is the mallard.

Mallard (Two Drakes)

The duck may be shot as part of a partridge or pheasant day when they have been flushed off a pond which is strategically close to a line of pegs that the duck may fly over. The duck may also be shot at the end of a game day at dusk when the Guns are strategically placed in blinds (concealment for the Guns) around a pond or lake to intercept the birds as they **flight** in to roost on the water.

Ducks are also shot around the coastline on the foreshore. Whilst still a game bird, this type of shooting is actually known as wild fowling. The wild fowlers may try to create a decoy by setting out dummy birds on an area of water in an attempt to attract similar species into that particular area. These wild fowlers will also strategically conceal themselves in blinds to try to intercept the birds as they fly to feeding areas. Geese also fit into the same season and generally are shot via the foreshore methods. Wild fowlers can extend their shooting season until 20th February by carrying out their duck and Goose shooting on the foreshore below the Spring Tide High Water Mark.

The reader cannot fail to notice that my description of this variety of game shooting is very short. I have participated in all of the types of duck shooting described, but have not done so for a long time and therefore it does not seem appropriate to write about it. However I wholeheartedly support all those who do choose to enjoy it.

1st September to 1st February - The Partridge

Traditional English Partridge Shooting

This book sets out to introduce and describe modern British game bird shooting. However, I am going to ask you to allow a little digression here - let me describe partridge shooting as it was traditionally done when the main partridge quarry was the indigenous 'English' or 'Grey' partridge. These were mainly wild birds blessed with an abundance of nesting, shelter and feeding habitats provided naturally by the then farming methods. Tall thick hedgerows and broad headlands (areas around the edge of fields) left largely untouched, free from harmful pesticides and abounding with crucial insect life was the norm.

On completion of the cereals harvest, the stubble fields were left fallow (unploughed) until the frosts of February. These stubble fields provided the perfect habitat for the Grey partridge where they were found in great numbers. Typical partridge drives would involve large numbers of beaters (the manual nature of farm work

(Left) A French, 'red-legged' partridge. (Right) Our native English 'grey' partridge

French partridges over a line of (lady) Guns

ensured that there was a large workforce perfectly placed to fill the beating line). These beaters brought in large areas of stubble that would produce covey after covey over the line of Guns, who would have been placed behind tall hedges. This would make for very testing shooting: Although these birds were not flying particularly high, they were only in view for a very short space of time, and being wild birds with a strong survival instinct they jinked and swerved in all directions.

Whenever the topography allowed, a further challenge was given to the Guns by placing them on pegs along the bottom of narrow valleys. With stubble fields along the tops and either side of the valleys, the beaters tested the skills of the Guns by flushing the partridges from stubble on one side of the valley, then later flushing them back from the other side (known as a return drive).

Shoots were very careful not to over shoot this wild stock; always ensuring that plenty of birds were left for breeding.

Tragically, intensive farming very quickly brought on the demise of our English partridge: Hedges have been ripped out, headlands ploughed up and widespread use of powerful insecticides has eradicated the necessary habitat and food supply. Optimistically, however, much work is being done in an endeavour to bring our native partridge back to sustainable numbers by reversing some of the intensive harsh measures that almost wiped them out. Also, on a very small numbers of shoots, English partridges are being bred and released, although this is a very difficult and expensive process. We must just hope the our little grey partridge will once again become part of modern British game bird shooting.

Modern Partridge Shooting

Meanwhile partridge shooting is being maintained by the rearing and releasing of the French or Red-Leg variety (a larger and more robust cousin to our grey, and one that is relatively easier to rear in the field). These birds are released as poults in pens much like our pheasant release programme (much more detail will be provided about this in the behind the scenes chapter when we look at the gamekeeper's year). These partridge pens are quite small and have covered tops to protect the young poults from winged predators. They are sited in cover crops so that the partridges start to associate certain areas as 'home' territory. These Red Legs provide a considerable challenge as they are flushed over the Guns in coveys, particularly when they are presented from cover crops on high ground.

Most shoots now have a stock of these partridges. This has added a new dimension to the driven game day as they have now become mixed in with the pheasants and fly over the Guns throughout the season.

The partridge is quite small in relation to the pheasant (about one third of its size). This small bird has a very rapid wing beat, therefore creating an impression of great speed. The larger pheasant gets to its optimum speed in around the initial 7 to 10 seconds of its flight, then glides creating an impression of moving slowly. In actual fact, it is moving quite a lot faster than the partridge. This mixture of the two bird species provides an extra challenge to the Guns, which is great for shooting.

1st October to 31st January – The Woodcock

Like the grouse, snipe and English partridge, the woodcock is a truly wild bird, but also a migratory bird (so not a true native). The exception to this seems to be small areas in the far South West that seem to maintain a resident breeding stock to a level that facilitates them having actual woodcock days when the birds are walked up and

sometimes driven over the Guns. I have not experienced this type of day, and have only shot the odd bird that has appeared over the line on a partridge or pheasant day.

There is a growing trend for shoot hosts to ask the Guns to refrain from shooting Woodcock in the belief that there are dwindling numbers. We all should always strictly adhere to any rules stipulated by shoot hosts; however, when I am acting as shoot captain, I invite anyone who chooses to shoot a Woodcock to do so providing that they eat it or are going to donate the bird to someone who will eat it. My own personal belief is that we are not going to upset the balance of the stock of a migratory population by shooting an occasional bird. I would also hate the thought that I had deprived any Gun of the opportunity to gain entry to the very prestigious 'Woodcock Club'.

The Woodcock Club

This club is administered by *Shooting Times Magazine* and to date has fewer than 1500 members. These prestigious few have gained their membership by achieving the remarkable feat of shooting a **right-and- left** at Woodcock (the right-and-left describing the situation of two birds being killed by two consecutive shots; the first from the right hand barrel and the second from the left hand barrel of a double-barrelled *side-by-side* shotgun) Although many of us are using *over-and-under* shotguns for our game shooting, we still use the term right-and-left. A right-and-left at Woodcock is remarkable because so rarely do two birds appear together in a way that would create an opportunity. The Woodcock Club rules are quite stringent in that they stipulate that 'the stock may not leave the shoulder between the two consecutive shots and the feat must have two reliable witnesses'.

Club members get to wear the special tie bearing a logo of four Woodcock pin feathers. They are also invited to attend a special annual dinner at a prestigious venue where they are each presented with a bottle of very special whisky. These annual dinners have also become very successful fund raising events for worthwhile shooting causes.

I have the honour, well more accurately the frustration, of very nearly being a member! A couple of years ago I was invited along with one other Gun, by a shoot owner to attend an informal **walk around** (walking with a few men with dogs to take the odd opportunity shots at game birds) very late in the season. We entered a large wood, where I was told to be the right hand Gun and to follow the fence line until I reached a clearing where I would see a pheasant release pen. My instructions were to wait at the edge of the clearing until the other two Guns and dog men appeared.

We were told to shoot cock pheasants, winged vermin (pigeons, crows, magpies and jays). Our host also permitted us to shoot Woodcock which he said were plentiful in this particular wood. Whilst walking slowly through the wood I could hear the others but not see them. I could hear the odd shot and was lucky enough to shoot a couple of pheasants and one Woodcock. I must also confess to missing two Woodcock in my excitement when I heard someone shout 'Woodcock: There are two of them!'.

I reached the edge of the clearing and waited as instructed. A couple of minutes had passed, when I looked up and saw two shapes flying towards me above the trees; I was looking at two Woodcock. Mounting the gun slowly, bang - first bird down! Bang - second bird down! Elation; I hear a voice (my own) shouting 'I just had a right-and-left at Woodcock'. Then I heard myself shouting 'Did anybody see?'. A dog man appears, and his two Spaniels pick the two dead Woodcock within seconds. The host appears, congratulations all round, but then the sad acceptance that no one has witnessed my right-and-left.

The next morning I felt that it is worth a phone call to the *Shooting Times Magazine*. I excitedly told a very nice lady. 'Yesterday, after 54 years of shooting, I finally pulled off my first left-and-right at woodcock!'

'Two consecutive shots without the gun leaving the shoulder?' she enquired. I was pleased to confirm this.

'Were the two birds picked?' she asked.

'Immediately,' I proudly replied.

'Did two people witness your success?' I quickly explained that there was a mass of circumstantial evidence and the very nice lady gently advised me that, sadly, I have not gained entry to the Woodcock club! She also concurred with my acid suggestion that 'I better try for another 54 years then'. So close and yet so far!

1st October to 1st February - The Pheasant

Cock Pheasant

Hen Pheasant

The fabulous pheasant: Fabulous not just because it is a large handsome game bird, not just because the high gliding curling pheasant presents one of game shooting's most challenging shots; but because it represents by far the greatest proportion of driven game shooting in Britain: Suffice, therefore, to suggest, that it is by far our most important and popular game bird. My own guesstimate is that there are currently around 500,000 people actively participating (shooting) on driven game days during the season; up to 80% of them are primarily participating on the 25,000 or so shoots that provide pheasants with some partridges. These shoots between them are staging around 150,000 driven days of varying sizes. There are probably up to 350,000 people making up the beating and picking-up teams actively involved in contributing to the production of these days.

As I endeavour to close this chapter, I realize that I am doing so on the last day of the game season (1st February) whilst I clumsily bash two fingers around the keyboard , those beaters, pickers-up and other shoot helpers are enjoying (or they have during the last few days) their hard earned keepers' day/s. Traditionally during the last few days of the season, gamekeepers organize special days so that everyone who has worked hard in helping to produce the driven days is invited to shoot on a walk and stand basis. These keepers' days normally involve shooting cock pheasants only, in an attempt to leave as many hens as possible as breeding and egg laying stock.

On completion of the keepers' days, everyone attending will be given a brace of pheasants for the table. So that is around 700,000 low-fat high-protein meals to benefit our food chain alongside the 15 million or so that already have entered the food chain during the season.

Chapter Three
A Brief General History

Whilst the pheasant is by far the most popular of our game shooting bird species, it is not a true native, although it has now been residing in Britain for a very long time. The consensus of historical opinion is that the pheasant was taken to France from its native Asia by Officers of the Roman Empire. It is believed that it was first brought across The Channel into Britain around the middle of the 11th century when it was viewed as an important culinary addition to dining tables and as a very handsome decorative bird. Its high culinary status appears to have remained stable right through to the late 16th, and possibly early 17th centuries. The popularity of the pheasant as a much sought after table bird appears to have been highest among senior ecclesiastical officers. Records have been found of the Archbishop of York's inauguration banquet in 1465 that state that 200 pheasants were on the menu.

Hunting for sport among nobleman and a privileged few has taken place as far back as records go. However, the history of the beginning of hunting the pheasant for sport is a little more vague. There are records that show that sitting pheasants were taken for sport during the very early 16th century by Noblemen using birds-of-prey. It is also considered likely that this style of hunting may well have been going on for much longer than the records show. It is also believed that some pheasants may have been shot for sport using crossbows during a similar period. Pheasants were also hunted for the pot during this period; using nets, snares, traps and longbows.

We know that Henry VIII, along with his courtiers and soldiers, had access to rudimentary matchlock muskets during the early 16th century, so it is assumed that shooting sitting pheasants with these firearms was the start of using guns to shoot game birds.

An artist's impression of Walked Up shooting using a Flintlock shotgun

By the mid-17th century, the flintlock muzzle-loading shotgun had become a fairly standardized gun and was commonly used by noblemen and gentry for shooting pheasants and the native English (grey) partridge for sport. These birds were shot walked-up - the Guns walked in a line through **coverts** (areas of woodland specifically planted to provide a hunting and shooting habitat) with their beaters and dogs, shooting the birds as they flew away. These coverts were often netted at the rear and sides to ensure that all the game birds that took off and flew forward to give most sport to the Guns. One of the main disadvantages of the flintlock was the fact that the explosive powder would spill out of the pan if the gun was angled too steeply so keeping the gun levelled horizontally at a walked up flying away bird, helped to maintain the efficiency of the weapon. Another style of Walked Up shooting of that era was to have the Guns on horseback with their servant loaders walking alongside them. When the beaters and dogs in the line

A 17th century Flintlock shotgun.
Courtesy of 'Beretta' via GMK Ltd.

flushed birds, the Guns shot from the saddle and then passed their flintlocks to their servants for reloading.

The Beginning of Driven Game Shooting

There are records from an estate in Northern Ireland that show that the owner held an especially grand pheasant shoot in 1674. The estate records show that 900 birds were in stock, and that this stock had been amassed via the natural hatch in the wild, combined with pheasants' eggs hatched under broody hens.

Seemingly, 64 guest Guns were invited to participate in the day, and it was recorded that between them they shot a bag of 300 pheasants. I find it very difficult to form a mental picture of 64 Guns all shooting at the same time on one estate; which at best strikes me as highly reckless. Interestingly, the records do not include any details about human fatalities or injuries. The fact that 64 Guns only managed to produce a bag of 300 birds would suggest that shotgun markmanship and bird presentation skills were lacking. It is likely that the owner of this estate had witnessed this battue (driven) style of show hunt in France, as these show hunts were fashionable on the continent, where they were used to demonstrate wealth, power and status. Regardless of the morals or purpose of this show hunt staged in Ireland, it almost certainly gave birth to the battue style of British game shooting that exists today. However the changeover to this style of shooting was a gradual one and did not start to get established until the mid 1800's, when the very slow to arm muzzle loading shotguns (that required gunpowder and shot to be poured down the barrels) were superseded by breech loading hammer guns (where a shotgun cartridge was quickly popped in to the breech).

The red-legged partridge was brought in from France to supplement our native 'grey' stock, although the game shots of the day viewed it as an inferior sporting bird. By the 1880s, British hammerless breech loading cartridge guns were in production; they were of a style and quality that is represented by the modern English *side-by-side* . Efficient guns, expanding wealth and great improvements in road and rail travel,

Pinfire Hammer shotgun made by Thomas Boss circa 1835. Courtesy 'Boss & Co' of London.

saw a growth in popularity of pheasant and partridge shooting; as the privileged few were able to access the large shooting estates around the country. Improvements in travel during the 1800's enabled much better access to the moorlands and highlands of Northern England and Scotland, fostering the growth in popularity of shooting the native red grouse in large number. This grouse shooting brought a massive boost to the income of these remote areas, as it still does today.

The Edwardian era probably brought about the greatest popularisation of driven game shooting. It became extremely fashionable to be known as a game shot, and the height of status if you earned a reputation of being an especially good game shot. The more birds you shot, the more you were respected. Huge bags were the order of this era, aided by the competitive approach of the attending Guns, most of whom would be **double gunning** (shooting a pair of shotguns, assisted by a loader) which resulted in a very rapid fire rate. Your reputation was greatly enhanced whenever you were seen to be shooting more birds than the other Guns in the line. Amazingly, bags of in excess of 1000 were commonplace and sometimes they exceeded 2000. The game books of the shoots that produced these huge bags record the numbers of birds shot and the feats of the 'notable' Guns in great detail; however, in most cases, it is difficult to assess just how challenging the birds were.

By the latter part of the 19th century, game rearing had become a fully established competitive commercial enterprise. Shooting estate owners were actively involved in the continual cross-breeding, including the importation of pheasants from different areas of the world, in an endeavour to produce the 'perfect' game bird. They strived to produce the most handsome bird that flew more strongly than others, bred more prolifically and was easier to manage. This search continues today.

Driven game shooting was very healthy in the early part of the 20th century, but then declined with the negative effects of two world wars, not least influenced by the reduction in fortunes of many of the shooting estate owners. These financial pressures, and the turning tide of public opinion, resulted in a drastic reduction of average bags from those enjoyed by the Edwardians.

The Growth of Modern Game Shooting

With dedicated commitment and investment from a few shoot owners, game shooting began a resurgence in the late 1940s. One such dedicated famous pioneer was Sir Joseph Nickerson. Alongside his own legendary personal shooting prowess (he was considered to be the most outstanding game shot of the 20th Century), was his single-minded determination to continually improve all aspects of British game shooting. His peers were convinced that he could think like any game bird. His shoots also produced some remarkable exceptions to the average 20th century bag sizes:

> *On 3rd October 1952; he and 5 guest Guns shot 2119 wild grey partridge on his shoot at Rothwell. Those six guns were each shooting triple guns served by two loaders.*
>
> *On 1st October 1959 the same six Guns shot a total bag of 2065 including 1877 partridges on the same shoot.*
> *Also at Rothwell; 4 Guns accounted for a total bag of 1940 including 1697 partridges.*
>
> *On Sir Joseph's Reeth grouse moor, on 15th August 1988 ; he and 7 guests shot 550 brace of grouse.*

Whilst the Edwardians huge bags involved birds of questionable challenge, Sir Joseph's feats (and those of his guests) resulted from phenomenally brilliant shooting of very challenging birds.

Anyone interested in game bird shooting should read Sir Joseph's wonderful book *A Shooting Man's Creed*. Whenever I look through it, I am always envious of his peers who were guests on his shoots and saw him in action.

Another positive influence for game shooting came about after the Second World War. On both sides of the Atlantic, pilots and air gunners were introduced to clay shooting as training for shooting moving targets (enemy aeroplanes). At the end of the war there were thousands of ex-servicemen who wanted to join the elite ranks of clay shots who had been enjoying the sport since the late 19th century. Most people involved in clay shooting at that time were using *side-by-side* guns, although Boss and Woodward, two of our most famous gun makers, produced *over-and-under* shotguns at the very beginning of the 20th century. These new style guns were of the same high quality as their best *side-by-sides* and were extremely expensive to buy. The high cost of these new *over-and-unders* combined with the British conservative resistance to change, resulted in most clay and game shots continuing to use their trusted *side-by-side*s.

These post war years saw everyone in severe austere times, so progress in clay and game shooting was quite slow for the general population. Many of the war time clay shooting trainees had been introduced to the flat single sight plane of the standard Browning semi-automatic shotgun and were aware that this single sight plane and other aspects of the *over-and-under*, made for a better tool to shoot with. They could not, of course, acquire the Best English *over-and-unders*; but did avail themselves of much cheaper imports from the USA and the Continent.

As affluence improved into the 1960s, some of the clay shots were curious and keen to further enjoy their shooting at game birds. Many of them got together and formed small self-help syndicates, and those that could afford to do so,

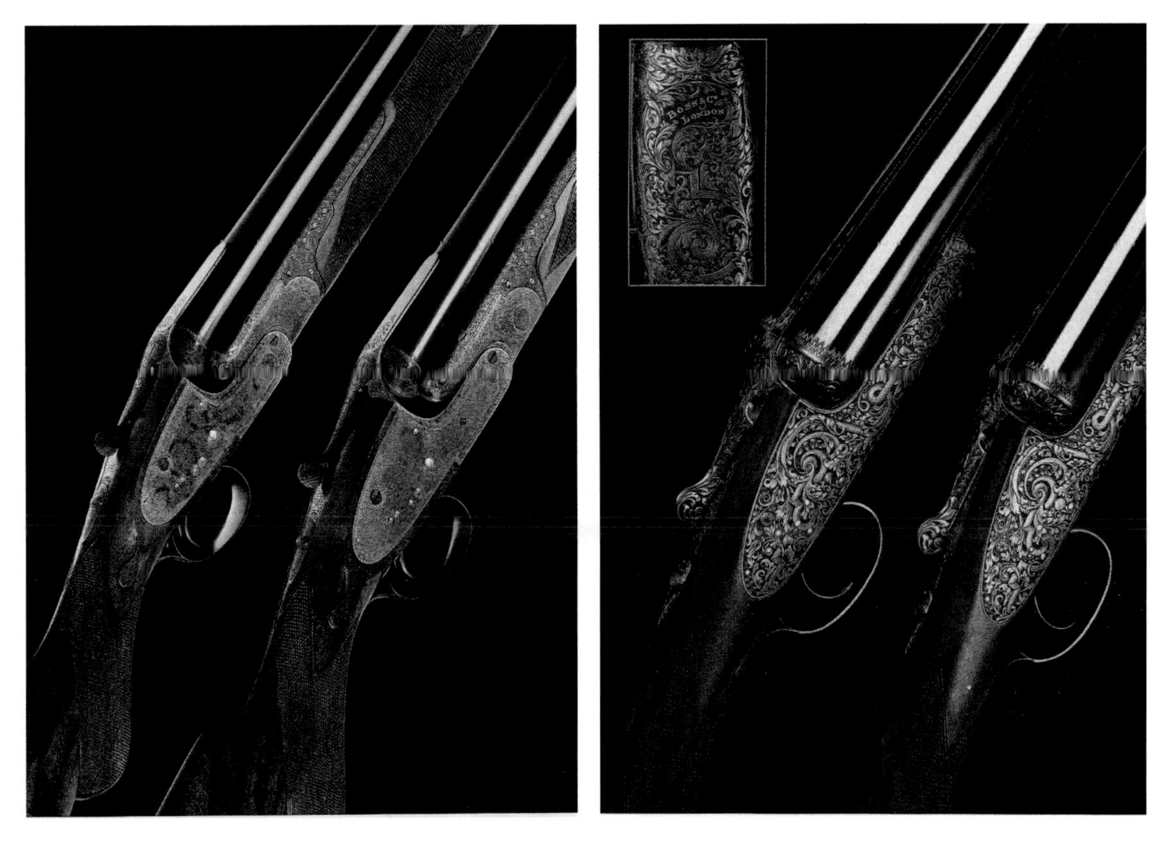

(Left) Pair of Boss & Co of London, sidelock over-and-under shotguns. 1912. (Right) Pair of Boss & Co Of London best quality sidelock side-by-sides. 1988, courtesy Boss & co. London.

joined more formal syndicates and/or took shooting via agents. They naturally took their *over-and-under* shotguns with them into the game shooting arena; so for the first time in our game shooting history, *over-and-under* guns were making an appearance on game shoots.

This is probably one of the main causes of the *over-and-under* being seen by traditionalist game shots as only suitable for clay shooting. Thankfully, this misplaced dogma has finally largely disappeared.

The greatest boost to shooting since Edwardian times occurred during the boom time of the 1980s. Suddenly, there were large numbers of very successful business people with plenty of disposable income looking for new leisure pursuits. Some took up yachting, some went motor racing, others went horse racing. Thankfully, many came to (and stayed with) game shooting. In addition to the extra income this brought into shooting, some of these newcomers became game shoot owners bringing their very positive and modern commercial attitudes and ideas into the rural field sports arena. Their considerable financial investment and determination to build successful shoots; following on from the efforts of Sir Joseph Nickerson and like-minded peers, has ensured the continued well-being and health of modern game shooting as it exists today. Shoot owners and hard-working gamekeepers deserve the credit for what they have achieved; however, a number of shooting organisations working closely alongside them, make crucial contributions to the game shooting success story. One such organisation that has provided so much beneficial research, is the Game & Wildlife Conservation Trust www.gwct.org.uk 01425 652381.

The GWCT is a unique charity that researches and develops ways of managing the countryside for the benefit of Britain's game and wildlife. The Trust's well-respected research has been critical in helping to restore our precious game and wildlife for more than 70 years. Their scientists have investigated the factors which cause the decline of wildlife and habitats. Once their research has identified a problem, they then develop novel solutions that work to reverse these declines. The Trust's findings are used extensively to advise farmers and land managers and are also used to inform policy-making decisions and lobby for conservation issues.

The GWCT also produces policy reports which identify measures that need to be taken in order to improve conservation efforts for game and wildlife. In their magazine *Nature's Gain*; the Trust examined the influence of game shooting and game management on wildlife conservation. Key points in this publication particularly highlighted the important role that game management plays in nature conservation:

- Moors managed for grouse have five times more golden plovers and lapwings as unmanaged moors and about twice as many curlews.
- From 1870 to 1970, pheasant shooting was a key motive for retaining and managing woods in lowland Britain.
- Management of woods for pheasant shooting results in higher numbers of song birds and woodland butterflies.
- Thousands of hectares of game crop and thousands of tonnes of grain provided for pheasants and partridges, help many song birds survive during Winter.
- Winter bird counts showed that there were often up to 100 times more birds in the game crops as there were in nearby arable crops.

I have been involved in field sports for well over 50 years; I believe that modern game shooting is now at it's very best, providing shooting that is more challenging and exciting than it has ever been. To ensure that you are up to the challenge; come back to the shooting school and let me help you prepare.

Chapter Four
The Method

Welcome back to the Shooting School. Now you know what a formal game day is, the different types of shooting that you might do, and have a little bit of knowledge about how game shooting started in Britain. We better start working together to ensure that you have the system, technique and skills to be a good game shot.

If you have read my latest book *Clay Shooting For Beginners And Enthusiasts* and/or watched my DVD *Shooting From Scratch* you will know that the system that I teach is referred to as **The Method** and if you have practised it, the next few chapters will be a valuable refresher.

Just in case you have not done all of the above, let me introduce you to (or refresh your memory about) this most simple system of shooting shotguns at flying targets (for the remainder of this book, now called **birds**). I choose to teach this particular system because my experience has shown me that anyone can learn the technique quite quickly. I believe that it is the most natural way for the human brain and hands to react because the pupil is encouraged to simply point at the bird; just think about it, most humans learn to point before they learn to walk!

Before introducing you to **The Method,** I fully accept that there are other systems of shooting that thousands of game Guns use to very good effect and, in fact, there is one that has been taught and followed for much longer than The Method. This system is loosely described as swing through and if you know that you use this system to good effect then stick with it - 'if it ain't broke, don't fix it!'. However, there are two parts of The Method that will prove crucial to whatever system you are using; more about that later. To clear up any potential confusion; it is probably worthwhile giving a brief description of the swing through system. Basically the pupil is taught to start with the barrels behind the bird, catch it up, accelerate in front of the bird (often described as 'swinging through') fire, and follow through (keeping the barrels moving).

Two old fashioned (but quite descriptive) ways of explaining this system were: 'Put the barrels on the smoke trail of the bird, rake the feathers of the birds belly with the bead, swing in front of the beak, fire and follow through'. Or, in the more basic vernacular: 'Bum, Belly, Beak, Bang!'

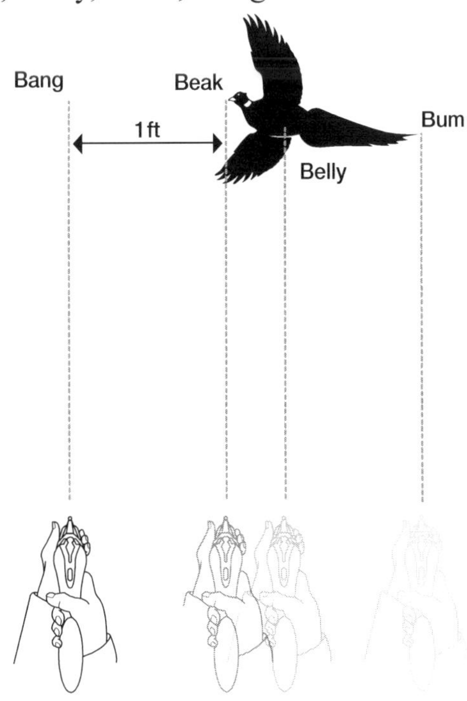

The "Swing Through" (also known as "Follow-Through") system

***NB** 1. Throughout the remainder of the book, bird silhouettes will be used in diagrams to represent pheasant sizes as they would be seen at typical game shooting ranges.*

2. Side-by-side users will quickly notice that the over-and-under shotgun is mainly used in the diagrams. This should not in any way be misinterpreted as any bias towards the O/U. It has been used to simplify the diagrams and provide uniformity. There are, however, specific instructions, accompanied by S/S diagrams to provide very important information to S/S users relating to shooting crossing birds at the end of chapter 5.

Now let us return to the Method and look at how we make it work when shooting a Driven bird; the pheasant flying straight towards us:

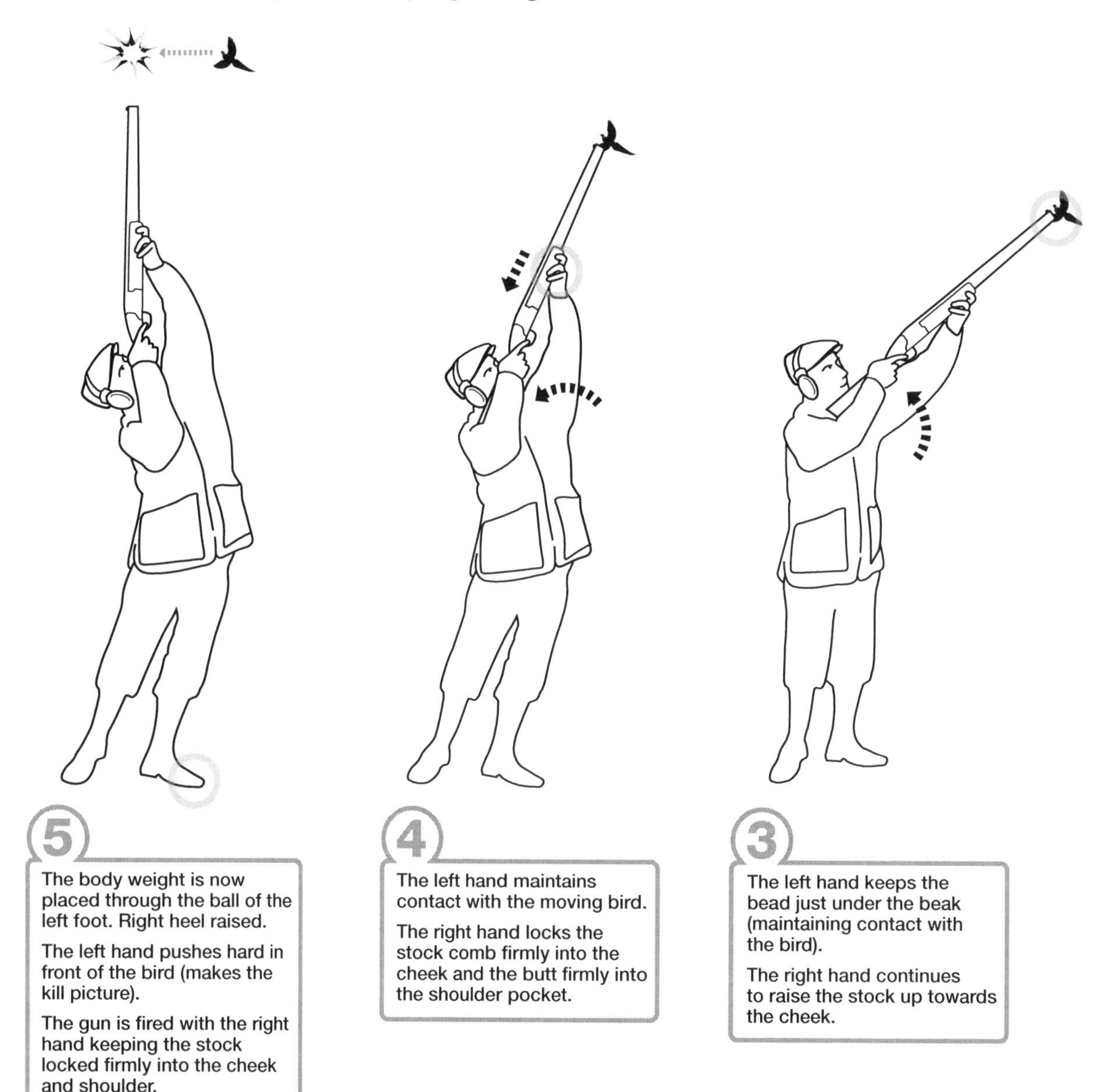

To get the best preparation for game shooting during the next few lessons, I need you to use your imagination and picture every clay target that is presented to you as a pheasant's head. Shooting The Method at game will always incorporate the actual physical process of gun mounting: controlling the timing of bringing the gun stock up, so that the **comb** (top of the stock) is embedded very tightly into the cheek and the butt of the stock is embedded into the shoulder pocket. These controlled twin movements are in tandem with pointing the bead just under the bird's head. I describe this embedding of the comb and butt as the lock. In any year's coaching, I would use the word 'lock' far more than any other.

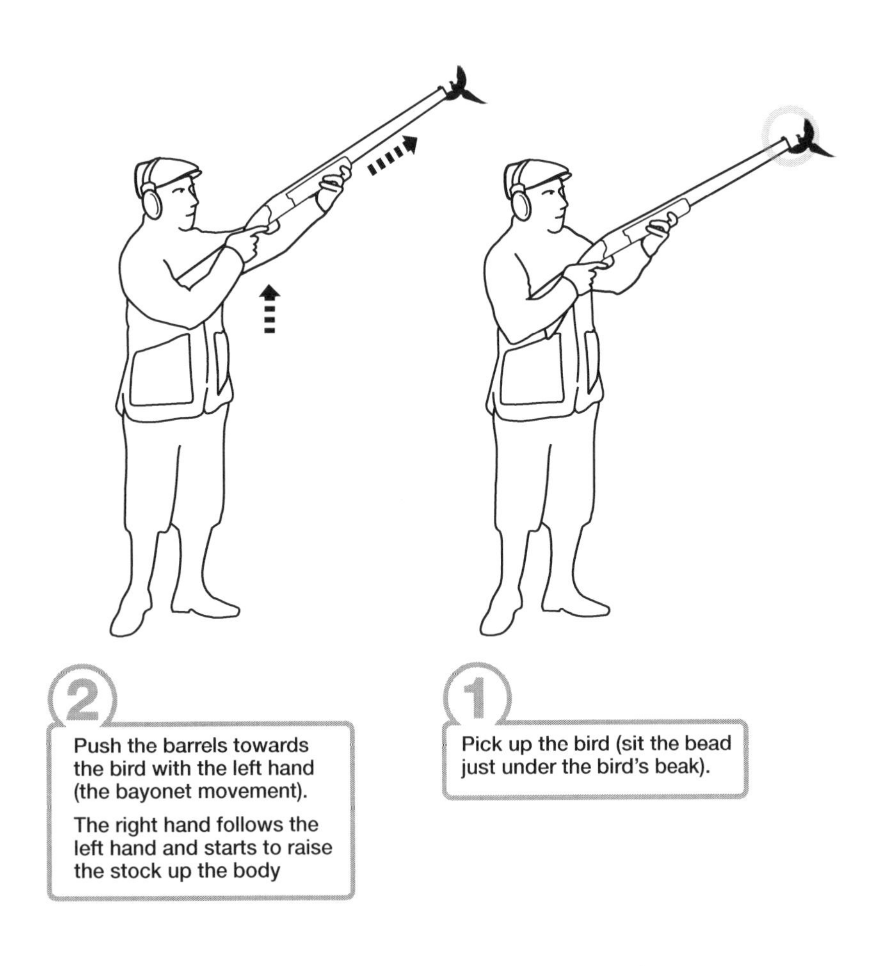

The sequence of gun mounting on a driven Pheasant

The timing of bringing the stock to the locked position, is as crucial as the lock itself and needs a great deal of practice; which we are going to begin on this Driven bird. You will first see it about 80 yards in front of you, above those young trees at the top of the bank, it will be flying over you at a height of about 60/70 feet (it has just occurred to me that we commonly describe distance in yards or meters, but almost always describe height in feet! I am not sure why we do this, but as it feels familiar I will keep to it).

Safety

Now to the first point of **field safety.** From now on, you must handle your shotgun as though you are stood on a peg on a game day. This means that you must behave as though there are beaters somewhere in front of you; therefore the topography dictates the safe angle that your gun barrels are held at.

Here we have a bank bearing trees in front of us, so your waiting gun ready position will always be with the barrels pointing above those trees. This is a crucial gun safety habit that must be ingrained in all game shooters, so that shot is never discharged into trees. When you are in the field you may have a bird flying that presents a sporting shot, but if that bird is flying across, rather than above some trees; do not ever shoot at it. The pellets from your shot could ricochet off a hard wood branch, particularly on an extremely frosty day. Staying with the safety theme, adhere to all the safety rules that apply when clay shooting, particularly, opening your gun when picking it up or taking it from the slip.

Until now, you could safely assume that if a clay was presented to you properly when you called 'Pull' it was OK to shoot. From now on, you have to have a completely different mind-set: you have to be sure that every shot you take is 100% safe before firing your gun. The golden safety rule in the field is simply: 'if in doubt; don't!'

One last comment on the safety catch. Clay shooting guns have 'manual' safety catches that can be pushed on and off whether the gun is opened or closed. Field shooting guns are designed with automatic safety catches that come on to 'safe' whenever the gun is opened. The traditional game shooting approach is to wait on the peg with the barrels at a safe angle with the safety catch on. When the Gun starts the movements of gun mounting to shoot a bird, the thumb pushes the safety catch forward to 'off' before the finger goes to the trigger.

The Physical Movements of The Method

Prepare to shoot your first Driven bird by applying yourself to the system of The Method. Earlier I mentioned that The Method involves a natural point. It does, but right-handers will be pointing their left hand and left-handers will be doing the opposite. As a right-hander, your first movement will be your left hand (remember to point your left forefinger alongside the gun's fore end) physically pointing at the bird as it appears, sit the pheasant's head just above the bead. This point is more than just a following of the bird; it is actually a very definite movement of the barrels towards the bird. Done correctly, it feels as though you are trying to poke the bird in the eye with your left forefinger. This first left-handed motion actually starts the process of the gun mount. As soon as this motion has begun, the right hand brings the stock up to the locked position. The visuals are: Sit the pheasants head just above the bead and keep it there. The timing is that the stock should only be at the final lock just as you are about to accelerate your left hand to get the barrels in front of the bird to allow for its movement. Ideally, when this bird is at an angle of roughly 70/80 degrees in front of you. For the sake of short sharp simplicity, I describe this controlled acceleration as 'push'. The push of the left hand is the motion required to create the right **kill picture** (often described as lead) which, on this Driven bird, is a picture of hiding the pheasant underneath the barrels. Yes, making a picture if you like of 'not seeing the bird', often described in shooting terms as '**blotting out the bird**'. Three short simple words describe this simultaneous set of movements using both hands: Point, Lock, Push. Point at the bird. Move with the bird. Push to make the kill picture. Fire! Really simple? Well yes it is really simple, if we can prevent the adult intelligent brain from over complicating it!

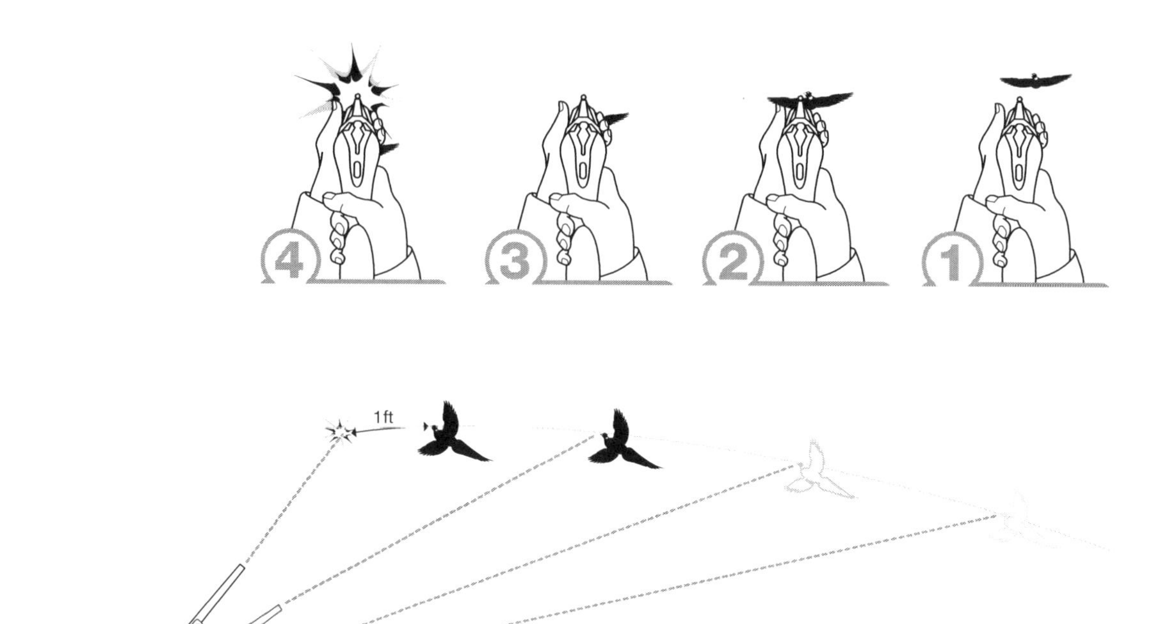

A Single Driven Bird

1. Pick up the bird

2. Point at the bird's head (move with the bird)

3. Push barrels in front of bird's head

4. Fire when your barrels have covered the bird'

Here is your first bird; point, lock push. Good, you killed it, but you worked much too hard and rushed the gun mount. Try another; good another kill, but slow that mount down; there is more time than you think. One more, nice and slow, don't lock too soon. Well done!

Pairs of Birds

Now try shooting some with the second bird appearing immediately as you have fired at the first one: Words of caution - take your time, try not to think about the second bird whilst you are shooting the first one!

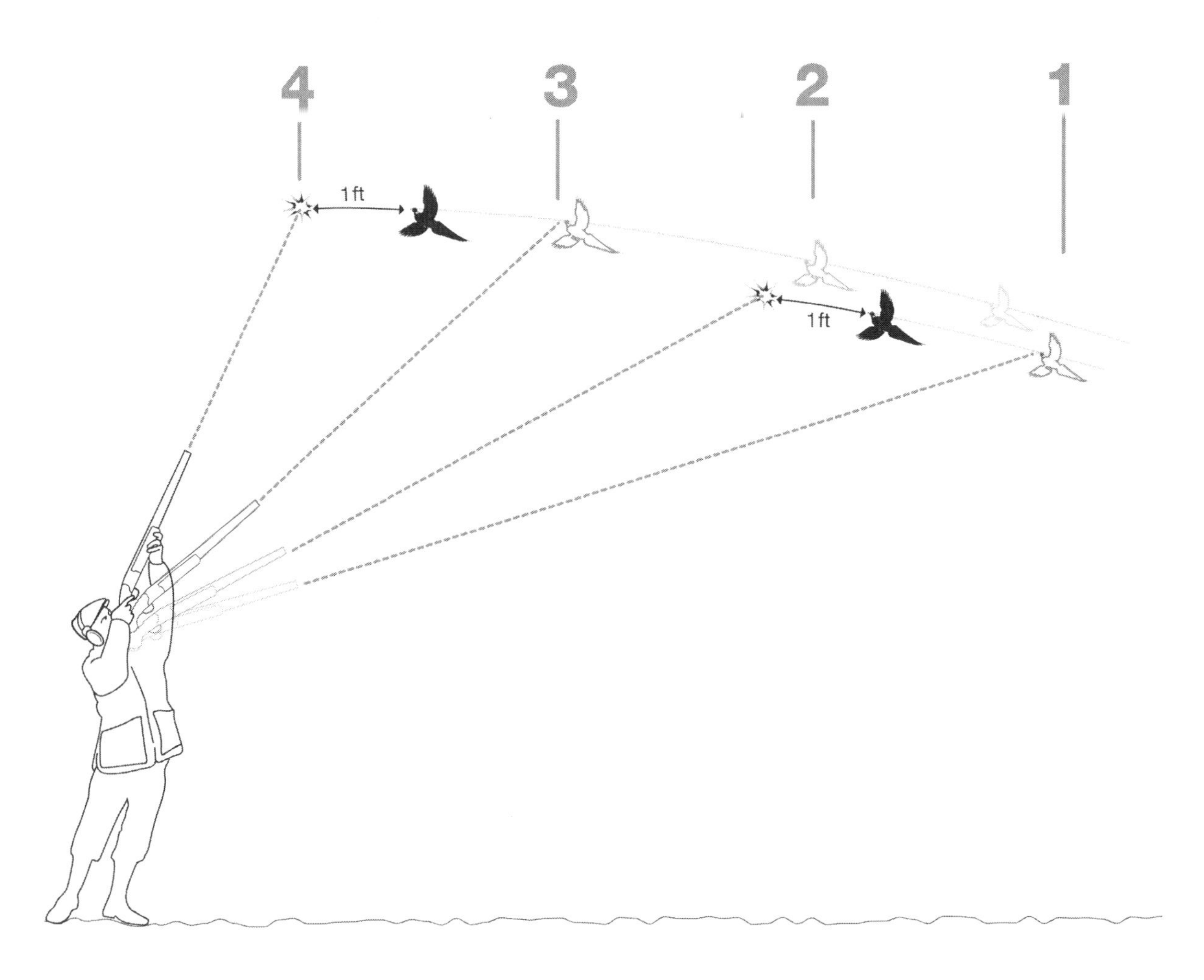

Shooting pairs (still described with the traditional term of "shooting a right & left") of Driven birds using The Method

1. Pick up rear bird
2. Pushing in front (blotting out) and killing first bird
3. Natural movement takes barrels onto second bird
4. Pushing in front (blotting out) and killing second bird

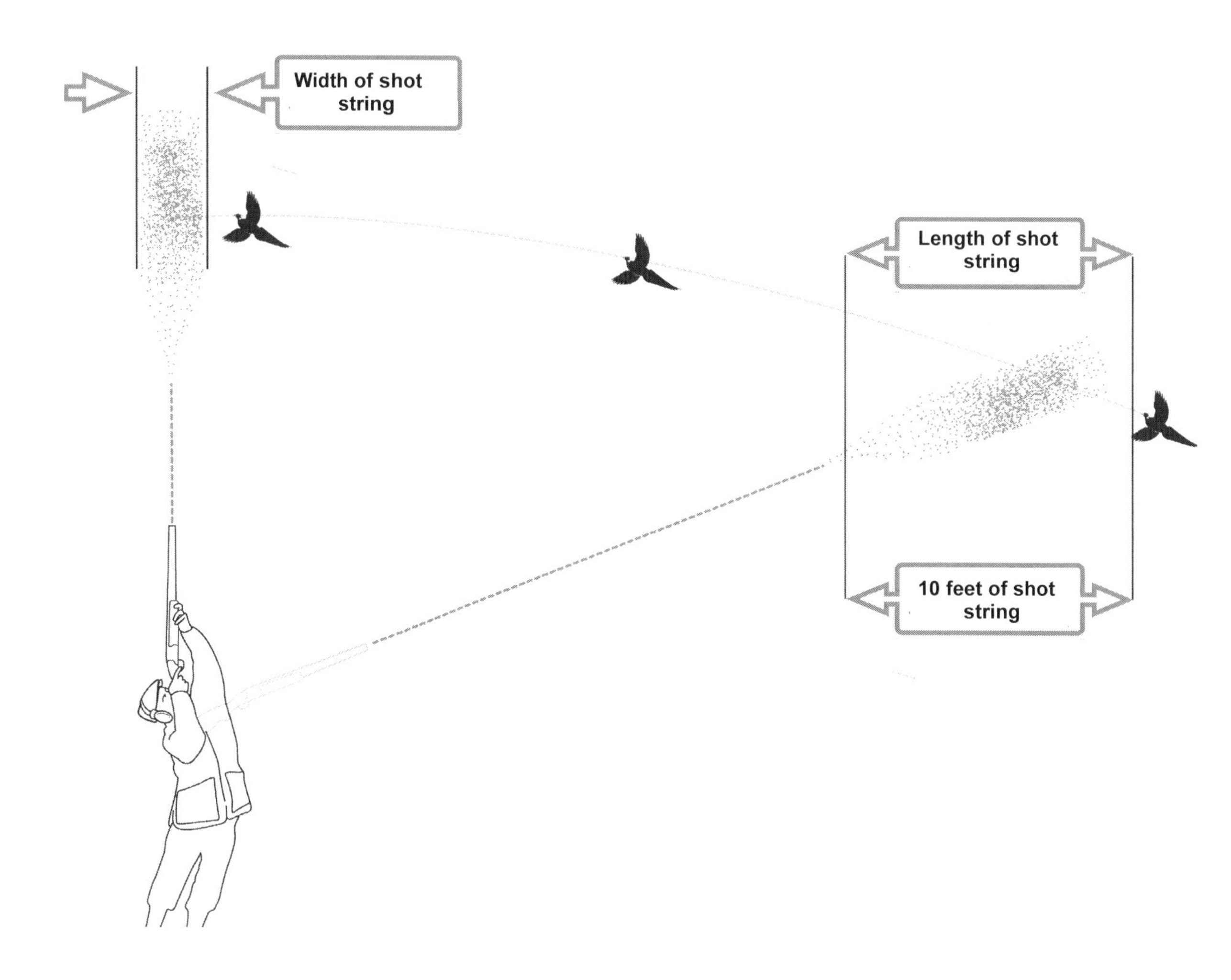

The advantage of shooting a Driven bird early

Off we go, OK so you missed the first bird, try again. Now you have missed both birds. Do not worry, this is typical at this stage. Only practice combined with the discipline to focus totally on the simple processes of The Method on each bird, will achieve success. Point, lock, push on the first bird with a slow controlled mount; then repeat that with exactly the same timing for the second. Now try some more; much better. The lesson here is that all pairs (right-and-lefts) must be treated as two separate jobs.

The next logical step whilst we are on Driven birds, is to look at taking two birds flying towards you simultaneously. When you are on your peg on a game day there might of course be more than two birds flying towards you; a flush of pheasants or maybe a covey of partridges (three or more birds flying together) More about that later; for now we will just look at shooting two.

First decision; which bird to take first? On this pair one bird is behind the other and I would suggest that is the one to go for. Point at the rear bird first. My simple reasoning is that as you push in front of that bird, you are automatically taking the barrels toward the second one.

More words of caution: In addition to the very natural instinctive feeling of needing to hurry the first shot (because there are now two jobs to do) there are two other initial difficulty factors:

1. Two birds in your vision simultaneously can be distracting.
2. Looking at two moving objects simultaneously can have a mesmerizing effect.

That is the theory dealt with; now for the practical. Here are your first two birds. The first one is dead but the other one escaped! You shot the first one far too late (remember that mesmerizing effect) so just could not get onto the second one. Try a few more. OK you are now taking the first bird earlier, but not yet connecting with the second one. Commonly, most pupils struggle on the second bird of the driven pair of birds at this stage: Let me explain the two main causes of this. Firstly, when we are getting on to the second bird there is not time to dismount the gun, so to get a clear pick-up we invariably lift our heads off the stock and have not re-locked as we are firing the second barrel. The other factor that causes regular misses behind the second bird is our failure to recognize that because this bird is passing over us at a steeper angle, it has a faster relative crossing rate and therefore needs more lead (more push). So, take the first bird early, ensure that you have the gun stock locked in very tight as you bring your barrels onto the second bird, then finally push aggressively in front before you fire.

There you go, it is very satisfying killing rights and lefts because it takes a great deal of determined concentration.

Crossing Birds

Not all of your game birds will be coming straight towards you, some will be incoming passing to your left and others incoming to your right. So now let us look at the bird crossing to the left. This is the easier shot for the right-hander, so we will master that one first: As always, there is a 'best' place to kill it. Too soon and you will be rushing. Too late and you will be making the shot difficult by winding in to an uncomfortable position. Also because you have been hanging on to the bird for too long, you will find it difficult to shoot naturally and instinctively.

An ideal position to shoot is when the bird is crossing between you and your neighbouring peg and is at about ninety degrees to you (we will look later at which birds are yours and which are your neighbours' in more detail).

This bird is at about the same height as the previous Driven bird and is going to pass at about 15 yards to your left. Having decided where you are going to kill it, you need to set your feet correctly (we will be looking at footwork and stepping around as we shoot later, for now we will settle for predetermined feet positioning).

Imagine that you are stood on a clock face and that the position where you have decided to kill the bird is twelve o'clock. Your left foot should be slightly in front of your right foot, with most of your weight being taken through the ball of the left foot. Your right heel should be slightly raised, helping you to push your weight forward naturally. Your feet should be placed at about five-past-eleven (depending on your stature, your heels should be roughly 8 to 12 inches apart). Before you take your shot, you will be winding your torso to your right so that your barrels are angled at a safe height and point at a position along the bird's expected flight path where you feel that you will see it clearly enough to be able to point at it early.

Your final decision in preparation is the kill picture. What you need to see relative to the end of the barrel, that tells you that you have allowed for the birds movement (forward allowance or lead in common shooting parlance). For the Driven bird you needed to push your left hand until you have hidden or 'blotted out' the bird with your barrels. For this crossing bird you need to 'push' until you see a kill picture that makes you feel that you are going to miss it about a foot in front. An actual recognizable gap between the 'bead' and the birds head.

Your gun mount must be that same controlled simultaneous set of movements that you practiced for the Driven bird. Remember that same initial 'poking in the eye' movement of the left hand to start the process of gun mounting and shooting The Method: Point, lock, push.

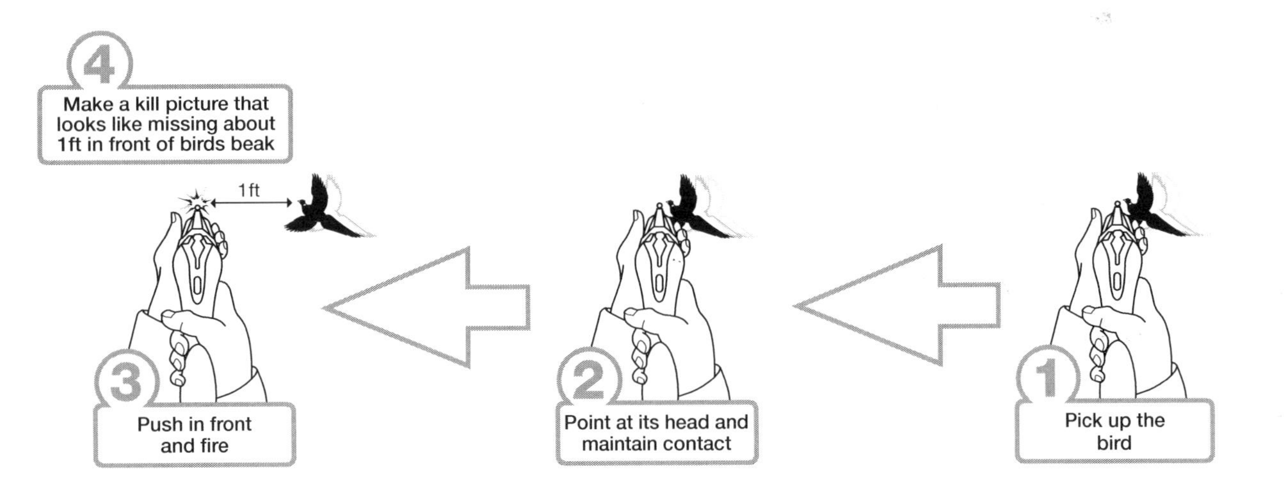

The Method applied to a right to left crossing bird

Now, set yourself up and shoot some: OK you have missed a couple, don't worry - your brain sometimes objects to losing sight of the Driven bird. Here it might well object to seeing a kill picture that feels like taking the barrels away from the very thing you are trying to hit. On the next one, just tell yourself to miss it a foot in front.

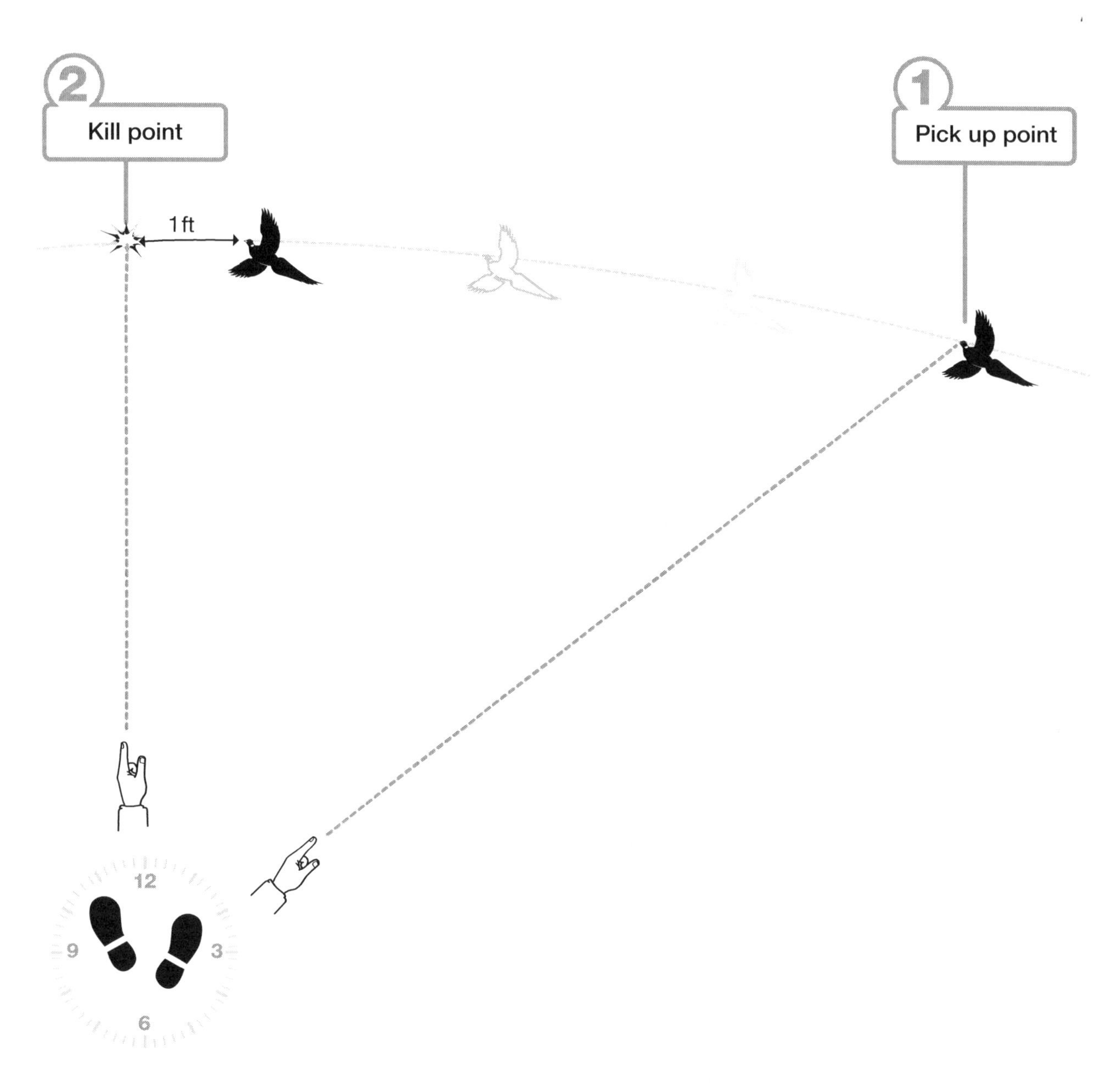

Feet position, pick up point and kill point for a single right to left crossing bird

That did the trick and you were killing them most of the time; you only missed when you forgot to stay 'locked', when you wanted to have a better look at your successes, and lifted your head off the stock.

A little tip, but an important one, when shooting any crossing bird - when you are pointing at the bird's head, sit the bead a little underneath it. Actually see a slither of daylight between the bead and the bird's head. Here is the reasoning: your gun (as are most guns) is built to put about two thirds of the shot pattern above your aim point. This is actually a very efficient design that we should be using to our favour. Pointing under our targets gives us a good clear visual image. So if we point underneath our birds we will have a clearer vision of what we are doing; we will have all of the shot pattern to strike the bird with, and we will be less likely to lift our heads off the stock.

Crossing Pairs

Now we are going to carry out the same 'doubles' exercises that we did with the driven pairs.

Similar words of caution: You will need to take your first bird a little quicker than you have been when it has been a single, if you are going to be able to take the second bird of your right-and-left at the best crossing point. Yes, you will have the same distraction and mesmerizing situation that you had with the driven pairs, and, yes, of course you will have the urge to rush your shooting because you know that you have two birds to cope with. Final reminder: Do remember, all pairs must be shot as two separate birds!

Just shoot a few and see how you get on, but be aware that when shooting the first bird earlier, it crosses you at a shallower angle than the second bird. Therefore the relative crossing rate is less, so it needs a slightly smaller kill picture. It needs less lead. You did very well, but did miss the first bird a few times, simply because you were tempted to rush.

Now let us look at the bird passing to our right. Doing the same singles then doubles exercises.

Everything is the same in preparation; remember you have a completely new twelve o'clock killing point, and therefore a new five past eleven feet position. You are going to learn two major differences here:

As a right-handed shooter you will always need to see more lead - 'a bigger kill picture' on a left-to-right moving bird compared to a right-to-left moving bird at the same distance angle and speed: Why? Simply because your normal right-handed body does not traverse your torso so naturally and efficiently around to your right. Most people take a little while to accept this; you will discover it to be a fact.

A right-hander shooting a left-to-right moving bird needs to lock the stock into his cheek extra tightly because as he starts to physically accelerate the barrels 'push' to his right, he actually forces the stock to come away from his cheek.

Time to shoot some; same height distance speed and angle than the right-to-left bird. I will stress again, much more lead; (about two feet). Plus an extra tight lock. Off you go. Five birds, five missed! Double your lead. Make a kill picture twice as big as the one that you have been making.

Here you go. Well done, you looked so surprised when you killed that first one. I know you were convinced that you were going to miss in front. But I hope that you are now convinced that 'left-to-right' always need more lead. Kill some pairs; you will have to make a supreme effort to stay locked in tight when you fire the second barrel because you left hand will be pushing the gun away to your right twice.

Well done, time to call a halt. Every right-handed person that I have coached has been surprised at how much harder it feels to master the left-to-right crossing bird. It just needs a great deal of practice.

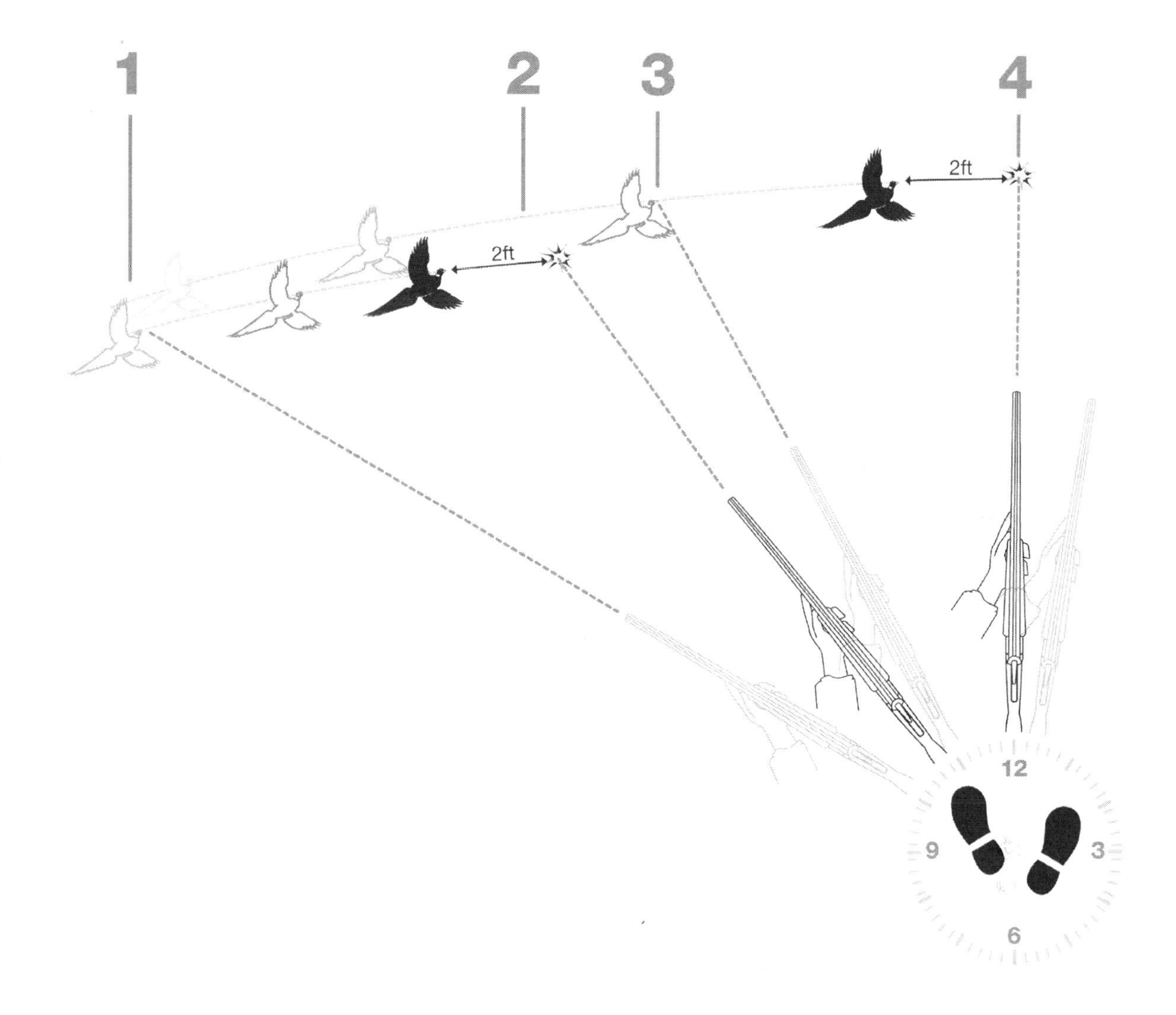

A right-hander shooting a left-to-right crossing pair of pheasants. Note; extra lead needed by a right-hander when shooting a left-to-right crossing bird

1. *Pick up rear bird first*
2. *Pushing in front of the first bird (making a kill picture that looks like missing about 2ft in front of the birds beak) and firing*
3. *Picking up second bird*
4. *Pushing in front of second bird (making the kill picture) and firing*

Gun Mounting Practice

On the subject of practice, I am going to give you some home work - something you can do at home without firing your gun. To shoot at your best level, it is essential that you practice your 'gun mounting'; everyone should. Those Edwardians that I mentioned in the last chapter used to practice their double gun changing and gun mounting with their loaders every morning before they went out to shoot pheasants in great numbers. They did this practice in front of a full length mirror so that they could see themselves carrying out all the movements correctly. This is what I am giving you for home work (although you don't need a second gun or a loader!).

Stand about six feet in front of a mirror where you can see a reflection of yourself from at least your waist upwards. Take a gun ready position so that the reflection of your right eye is sat just above the bead of your gun. Now start the movements of gun mounting, with your left hand taking the barrels towards the reflection of your right eye. Complete the process of mounting, bringing the stock up to be locked into your cheek. Initially, you should carry out these movements very slowly, gradually speeding them up.

Your prime objectives are to ensure that the reflection of your right eye stays visible just above the bead; and that your head stays completely still as you bring the stock up to the locked position. This practice will not be the most exciting thing that you ever do; however you will really benefit if you can discipline yourself to spend just a couple of minutes gun mounting in front of a mirror a few times every week for the next six months. Remember those Edwardians shot prolifically, and they did so very competitively; they really understood the crucial importance of good gun mounting!

During your next lesson we are going to focus on shooting reactively at birds being presented to you at different angles, which will involve your introduction to good footwork.

Practice gun mounting in front of a mirror

Meanwhile, I will leave you some notes on The Master Eye:

Eye Dominance

'Should I shoot with one eye shut or both eyes open?' - yes, that old chestnut. I am still regularly astonished when pupils tell me that someone (could be a coach!) has told them that they must keep both eyes open for successful shotgun shooting. This outdated belief is still being forced, quite dogmatically, onto so many unsuspecting novices. Just yesterday I had an e-mail from someone in New York who watched my DVD and decided to ask me for clarification on the 'one or two eyes' question. This novice had been told to shut the left dominant eye by one coach, and later had been told that 'both eyes must be open' (I mention New York simply to reinforce the global extent of the problem).

Please let me provide a simple explanation: Firstly where does this 'both eyes' come from? I suspect from an era long ago when a privileged few were shooting game that was mainly shot 'walked up'. So youngsters being trained for shooting were taught on targets that were flying away from them. The belief was that any one being allowed to shut one eye would use the shot gun like a rifle and therefore 'aim'.

The modern reality is that about 50% of shot gun shooters (clay and game) shoot with one eye shut and many of those are extremely good shots. The majority of those who shoot with one eye shut do so because they have the wrong dominant eye (in the simplest of terms, right-handers who have a 'master' left eye and vice versa for left-handers). These people have learned that the easiest solution to having the wrong master eye is to shut it as soon as they have a clear pick up of their target. My practical experience has shown me that roughly 40% of males and 90% of females that I coach have the wrong dominant eye (no, I don't know why there is a difference between the genders; and I am not lying awake at night worrying about it!).

In addition to those who have the wrong dominant eye, there are a few people who only see a definite kill picture with one eye shut, there is also a tiny percentage who have exactly equal vision in both eyes. On the basis that our brains are not consciously aware of which eye is sending the command signals to it; those with equal vision can get very confused if they do not shut the non-shooting eye (right-handers need to shut the left eye).

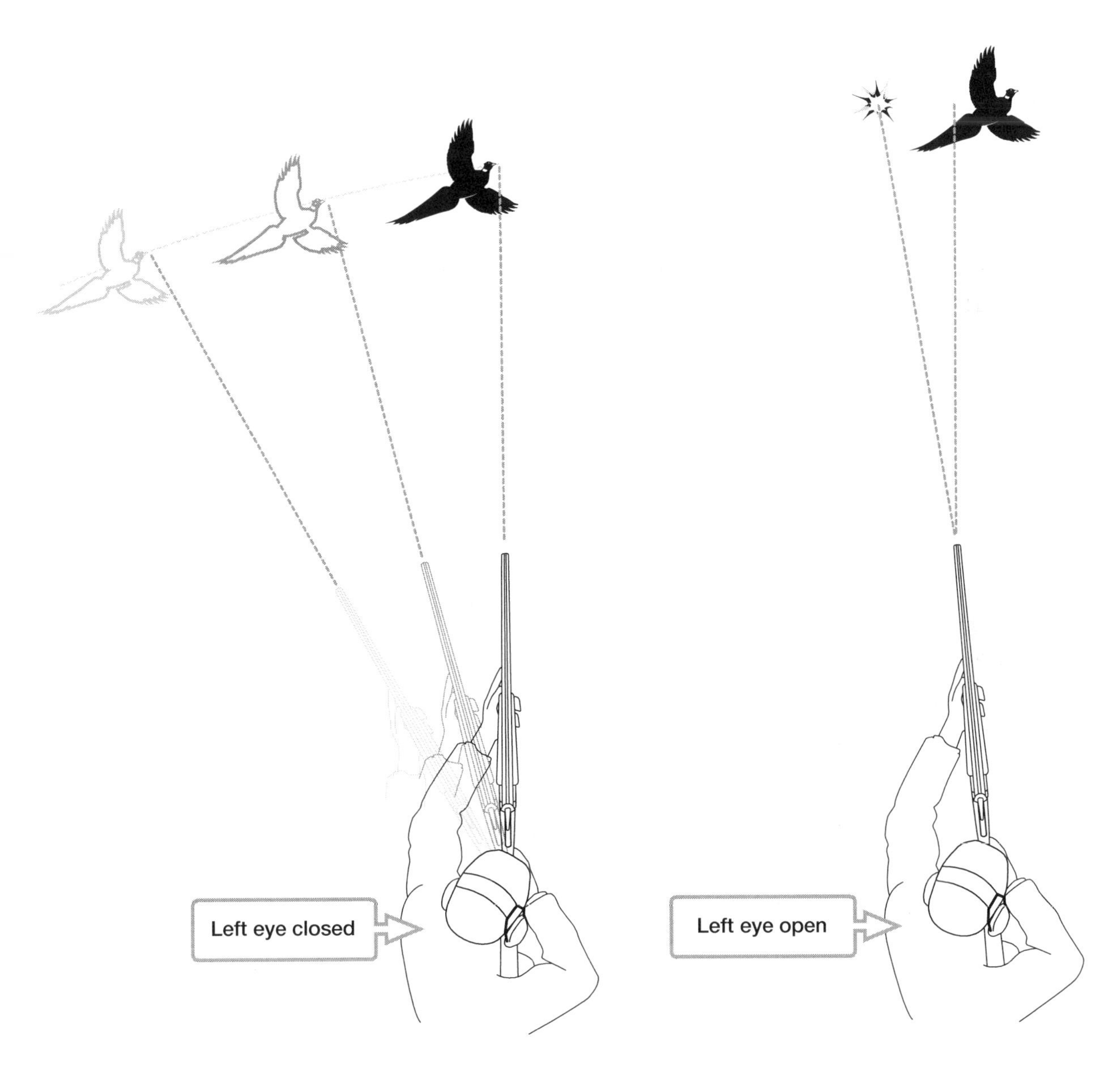

A left-eye dominant shooter tracking a left-to-right pheasant with the left eye closed and the left eye open

A few people with the wrong dominant eye have a dominance that is so strong, that this eye will not close. There is a simple solution in the form of shooting glasses that have 'insert lenses' that defuse and/or reduce the vision in the dominant eye and improve the vision in the other eye. Learning to shoot off the other shoulder is an option, but one that I feel is too extreme. Of course, shooting with both eyes open provides advantages: Two eyes will send more efficient optical signals to the brain than one eye, and binocular vision makes it more natural and easier to judge distances. I shoot with both eyes open, but that is just luck. I am right-handed and right eye dominant so am quite comfortable shooting with both eyes open.

Words of caution to you long-term experienced shooters: If you inexplicably find that the standard of your shooting deteriorates; pay a visit to your local shooting school. It is possible that your eye dominance has changed and this is quite common with advancing years.

Follow Through - Explanatory Notes

Professional coaches, and some experienced shooters, will have noticed the omissions from the text and diagrams of the term 'follow through'. This is deliberate, but of course warrants a full explanation. Many years ago, I was introduced to the 'Method' system of shooting on my first Clay Pigeon Shooting Association Coaching training course. I was an immediate and enthusiastic convert to this wonderfully simple system of teaching beginners to shoot moving targets with a shotgun. The CPSA Method included 'follow through' as the final movement of the gun after firing; which I slavishly followed for many years. However, thankfully, I continue to learn and, a few years ago, it occurred to me that teaching novice pupils to 'follow through' actually created an unnatural and unnecessary movement. Yes, the gun is kept moving at the time of squeezing the trigger, however I now believe that if The Method is adhered to, the gun will follow through naturally. Here is my logic: When the shotgun is pointed at a moving target it is naturally moving at the appropriate relative speed. If the relative movement of the gun is sped up to make the correct kill picture (pushing in front of the bird to create lead) and the trigger is squeezed on the recognition of that picture; the gun must come to a gradual and natural stop.

In simple terms the barrels have 'followed through' quite naturally without any extra or artificial mental or physical actions being required. While I continually hear, 'I/he/she stopped the gun', it is my opinion that rarely does anyone 'stop the gun'. However I do understand why people think that they have.

When attempting to make a kill picture (lead) it is very common adult reaction to try to make that picture precisely correct. This often results in a fractional moment's hesitation. Conscious intelligence is checking the kill picture. I call this 'play back time', hardly measurable, but enough to cause a miss behind the target.

If you are a novice pupil, or maybe you are an experienced shooter trying to help a beginner; I would encourage you to forget 'follow through'. Focus on squeezing the trigger immediately on recognition of the kill picture. Trust the hands and avoid the precise approach. Remember kill pictures are always approximate.

Chapter Five
Shooting Reactively - Footwork

Welcome back for another lesson. Now that you have the movements and sequences of shooting the 'Method' as a solid foundation; you will be able to build up your skills quite quickly.

You are quite competent at shooting birds driven towards you and incoming, passing to your left-and-right. However, so far you have known the angle at which the bird will be presented to you, and have had the luxury of pre-preparing.

Now I am going to show you how to respond to the bird in the air, and shoot it reactively, which will require good footwork. Here is where you will discover that game shooting is definitely 'a whole body sport'. We will start with the Driven bird which requires the minimal amount of footwork. When you were waiting at the gun ready position for the Driven bird that you were expecting; you had pre-set your feet. Left foot slightly in front of the right foot, with the right heel slightly raised. Feet set at about five-past-eleven.

From now on, set your feet much more naturally when you are waiting at the gun ready position. When the Driven bird appears and you make that initial point of your left hand, take a natural step forward with your left leg. It is just one small step forward so that your body weight is transferred naturally through the ball of your left foot. This weight transfer is completed with a slight raising of the right heel. Whilst carrying out these very simple minimal feet movements, your hands complete the movement and sequence of shooting The Method; point, lock, push.

Time for you to try some: Remember to stand with your feet placed comfortably and naturally. Your left foot is not going to move until you have picked up the Driven bird and have started to point your left hand at it. Just shoot a few; no it will not feel totally natural until you have practiced the movements. Shoot some more with birds coming at you in quick succession. You must remember to step back to a natural stance after each shot ; your feet will only react correctly if you are starting from a comfortable natural standing position. You must have a starting position to move from.

I am aware that this seems like a great deal of words to describe a minimal simple movement and introducing footwork feels like having more to do and think about. I promise you that, with practice, it will soon feel completely natural and will definitely result in the most efficient use of your whole body when you are shooting.

You may not be aware that your current need for extra thinking results in you failing to shut your left eye, which you long ago decided suited you best.

Let me add two more simple words to your method sequence - 'shut' and 'step'. So now your sequence is: Point, shut, step, lock, push.

Point your left hand, shut your left eye, step with your left foot, lock the stock into your cheek, and push in front to make your kill picture. Fire. Job done! Shoot some more, saying this new five word shooting sequence to yourself. Well done. You have discovered that it starts to feel natural quite quickly.

In my search for simple everyday analogies I used to suggest that pupils should take a gun ready position with a stance that felt like 'waiting for a bus' and the initial point of their left hand and little step forward could be likened to signalling the bus to stop. The other day, I made this suggestion to a pupil who looked horrified and exclaimed indignantly, 'I don't use buses, I always use taxis!'. So, your new gun ready stance and initial movements for shooting on the peg are just like 'Hailing a taxi'.

Footwork for The Incoming Right-to-Left Bird

The next task is to get to grips with a reactive approach to shooting the bird passing to your left. You discovered the best place to kill it when you were practising The Method on it previously, so that was where you needed to step your left foot to. Stepping to the left is going to take a little more thought, effort and movement, than stepping to the Driven bird; and deserves some further explanation:

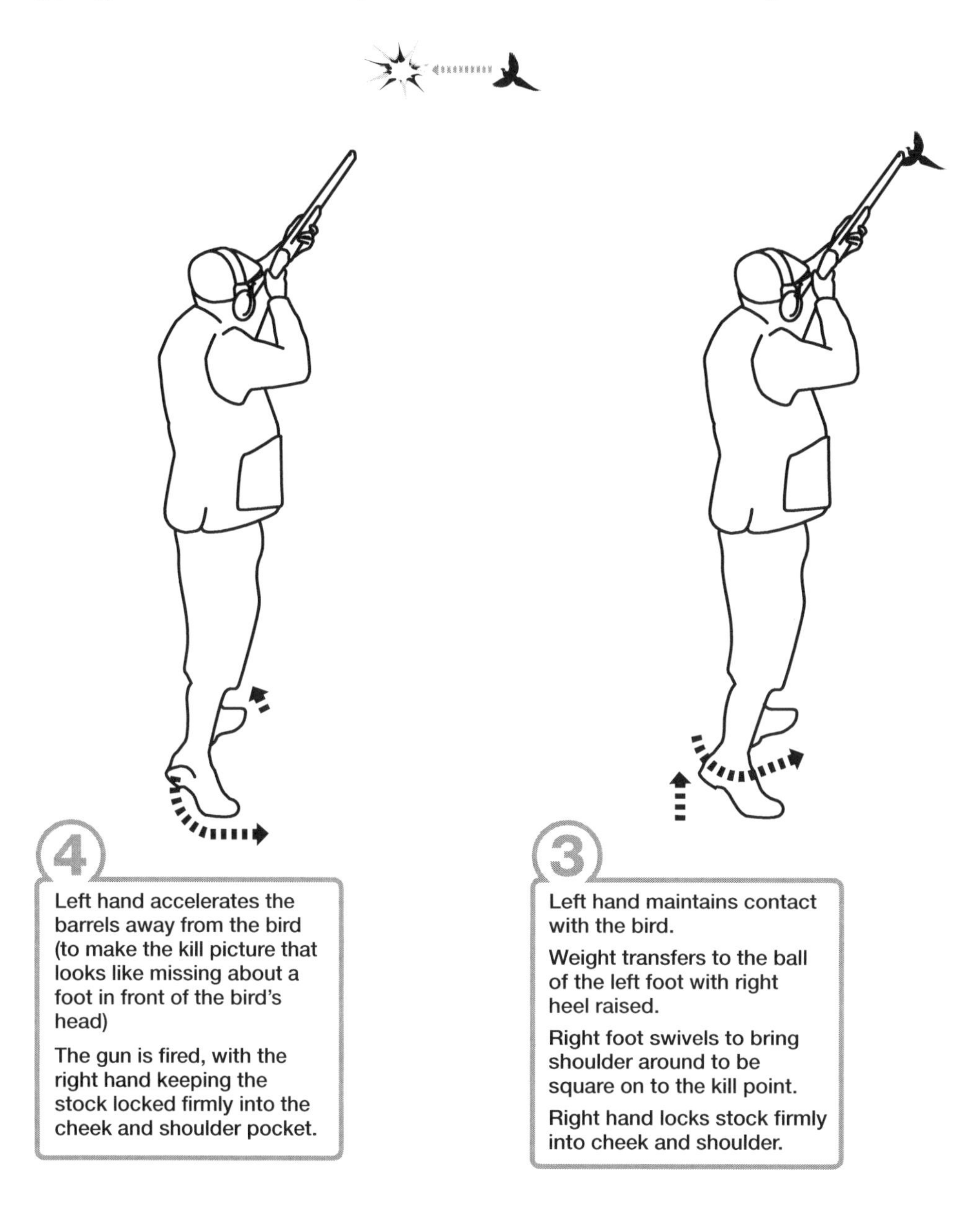

Firstly as your left foot steps around to the left; your torso naturally follows. It is anatomically obvious; but it needs stating, that as your arms and hands are attached to your torso, they will also naturally follow around to your left. This will result in your gun being a long way in front of the bird. Logically you are going to need to learn another small addition to your sequence of body movements: You are going to learn to metaphorically disconnect your left hand from your left foot.

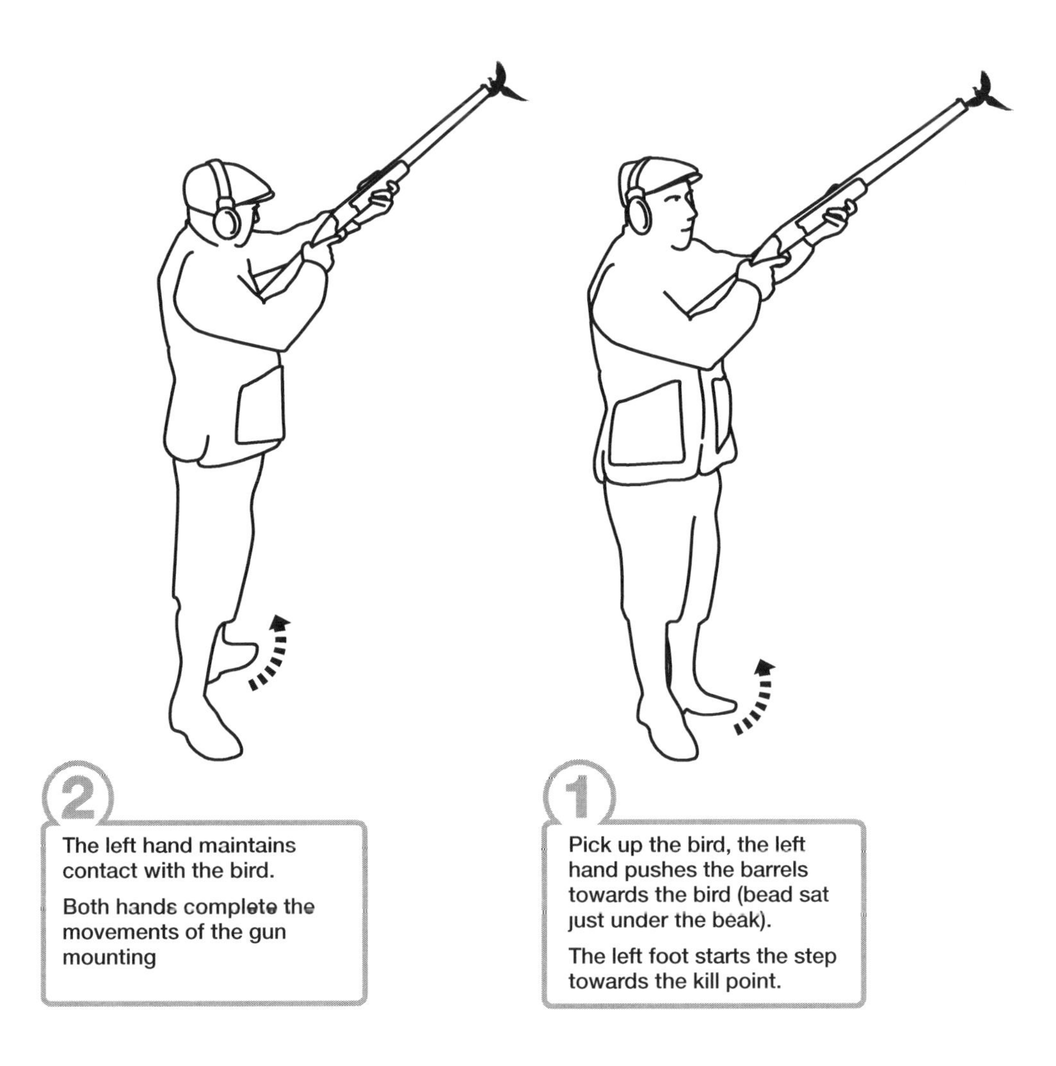

Footwork for the right-to-left crossing bird

Put your gun down, because before we can progress, this needs practice. Just stand naturally and point your left forefinger at this bird as soon as you can see it clearly. As soon as you start to point, shut your left eye and start stepping your left foot around to the kill position. Yes, I know it feels a little awkward at this stage, because your left hand wants to go with your left foot. Just keep practising. You just have to get used to the strange initial sensation of your left hand and left foot pointing in different directions. You will eventually get to feel comfortable with this.

Now to add the final body action that completes this movement, which involves your right foot. When you were stepping to the Driven bird, your right foot simply had to gently raise at the heel. It will still need to do this, but will also need to swivel to the left on its ball as the heel raises. This final tiny action is crucial to completing the whole body efficiency motion of stepping to the left hand bird; because the right foot swivelling to the left brings the right shoulder around to be square on to facing the kill position. This is essential for maintaining a tight lock of the gun stock.

Try this straight away: No gun or moving targets are required for now. Just step your left foot around to the left and, as you transfer your weight, raise your right heel and swivel on the ball of your right foot. Feel your right shoulder moving naturally around to be square on to where you are now facing. Step back around to where you were first facing and do this little exercise once more.

This time turn your head to your right so that you look at your own right shoulder. Note how that little swivel on the ball of the right foot brings your shoulder around so easily and natural. (I hope that you readers are doing this little exercise. If you are reading on a train or aeroplane you will need to stand up. Yes you might feel a little odd, but just think how much your shooting is going to improve!)

More rehearsal, pick up your empty gun and slowly practice the stepping movements and simultaneously mount to an imaginary bird. Now, still using an empty gun, practice on some birds incoming and passing to your left. That is enough; time to shoot some. Remember to step back to your original feet position after each shot. Well done, but this aspect of your shooting needs to be practised regularly until your movements become totally instinctive.

Footwork for the Left-to-Right Bird

When you were practising on incoming crossing birds, you discovered that getting to grips with the left-to-right required the most work. This will be the next bird that you are going to shoot reactively. In doing so, you will realise how important good footwork is.

In order to get your right shoulder square to your new twelve o'clock kill position, your left foot will need to step a long way around to your right. As your weight starts to fall forward onto the ball of your left foot, your right heel raises and swivels left, both to maintain your balance and keep your right shoulder square to the kill position. This is the most your feet are going to work when you are shooting in the field, and therefore needs the most practice.

Try the stepping of the left foot around to your right and raising with swivelling of your right heel. Now let me present you with some clays as incoming left to right birds. Just practice pointing your left forefinger as you try out the stepping exercise. Carry on this practice, using an empty gun. When you are ready, shoot some. Final words of caution: These feet movements should not be felt as fancy dance steps, they should be a deliberate natural walk to where you have decided to kill the birds. You may feel a little clumsy at the moment, keep trying and remember that these birds to your right need more lead and a very tight lock.

Take a breather before you make the next natural progression to shooting totally instinctively.

I will present you with clays at random from different angles so that you can practice your reactive shooting as you would need to do at birds from your game peg. A totally different approach to shooting than what you have previously practised. It is also great fun, which of course shooting should always be!

1

Pick up the bird, the left hand pushes the barrels towards the bird (bead sat just under the beak).

The left foot starts the step towards the kill point.

2

The left hand maintains contact with the bird.

Both hands complete the movements of the gun mounting

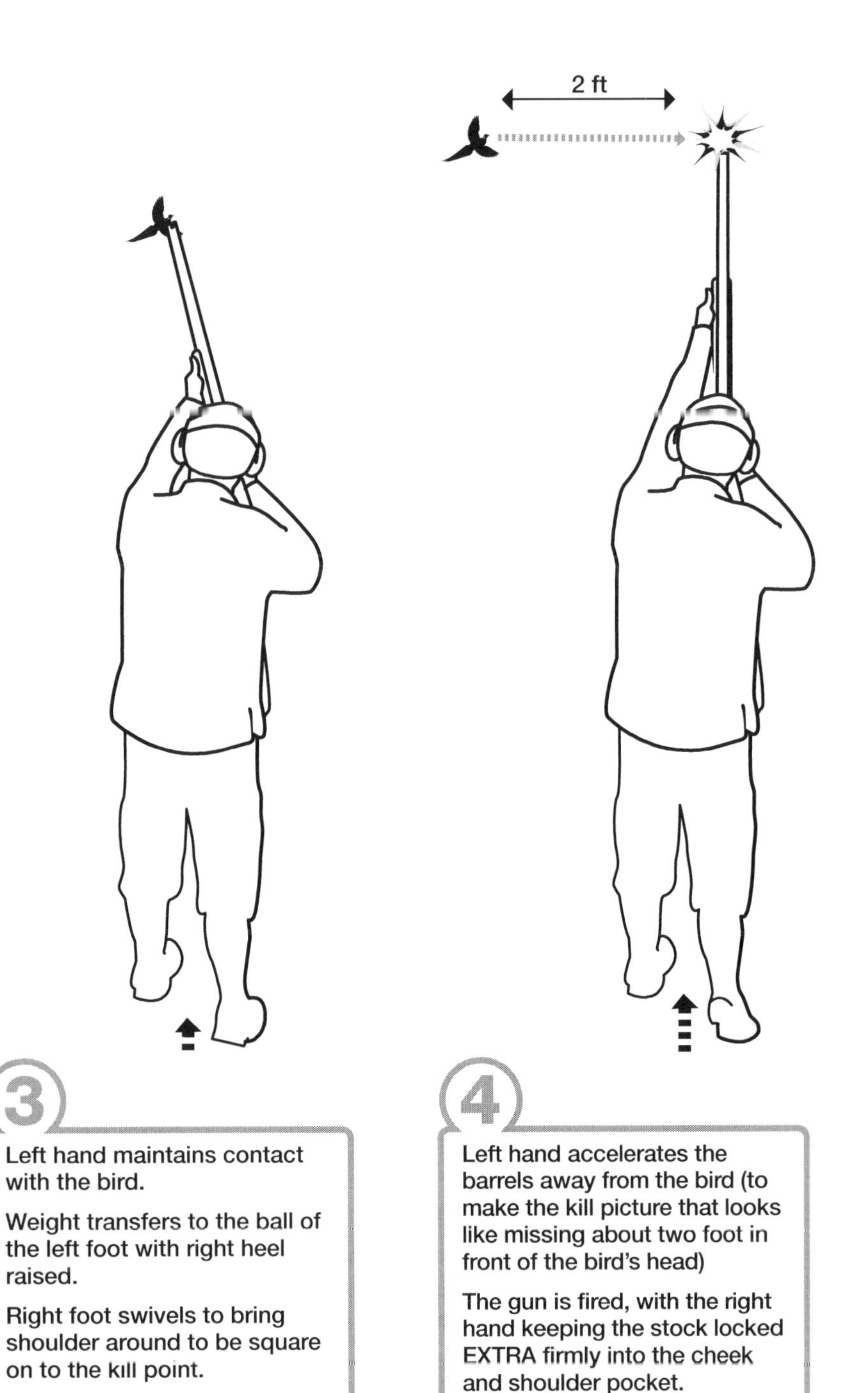

Footwork for the left-to-right crossing bird

Reacting to Multiple Birds in the Air

Time for a new exercise which I hope that you will also find to be enjoyable. A while back I warned you that you would be likely to be faced with three or more birds flying towards you. You also learned that just two clays in your vision is distracting and could mesmerise you. Now we are going to add to that challenge by presenting you with four or five clays in the air simultaneously (a flush of pheasants or covey of partridges may well be more birds than this number of clays, but this is sufficient for this exercise).

Firstly, I am going to stand you where the birds will be driven straight over you, then I will move you to either side so that they are passing to your left and latterly, to your right.

Have a blast and see how you get on. OK you had fun as I hoped you would, but a few points whilst you rest. Yes, of course you were distracted, and the more excited you became, the faster you tried to load and the more you forgot about what you have been learning. Although these 'birds' are coming from machines, always put safety first and keep your barrels up at a safe angle! Take a simple and logical approach as to which birds to take - always go for the ones flying closest to you. If a covey of partridges flew over your peg and you shot at the birds nearest you, your peg neighbours would feel free to shoot at the birds nearest them. Likewise if a covey flew to your right or left and you shot at the ones nearest you, hopefully you would not have deprived your neighbours of shots of birds driven over them. Do slow down, pick out just one bird and concentrate on shooting The Method. Stay focussed on the process rather than the success (yes of course the success is the 'buzz')

Try some more. Well shot, it is all starting to click into place.

Footwork for Turning to Shoot Safely Behind

During this session, I have placed a great deal of emphasis on good footwork; this seems a convenient juncture to add one more exercise where good footwork is essential. In chapter two I mentioned shooting in a grouse butt and described situations where for safety reasons the birds had to be shot behind the butts. I also commented about partridges being presented to the line of Guns over hedges. There are going to be occasions when partridges fly over you (singles, pairs and/or coveys) when, for safety or good sportsmanship reasons; it is inappropriate to shoot in front. However the bird flying away behind you can make a testing sporting shot.

In your first season, you may not have the confidence or opportunity to attempt this shot, but I know a great many very experienced game shooters who could benefit from this lesson. If I had to highlight a weakness amongst our best game shots it would actually be this 'taking the bird behind' Why? Because they have never included it into their repertoire of pre-season sharpening up; and they are not presented with this particular type of shot very often.

Let us show all of those old hands how to go about it: Here is a clay coming towards us representing a low flying partridge or grouse (we do not try to take a pheasant flying straight away behind us, as the bird's size, and tail feathers may prevent a clean kill). Having made the decision to take it behind us (only if we are 100% certain that there are no pickers-up anywhere in that vicinity), we drop the gunstock down low so that the barrels are as near to vertical as is safe . The barrels are kept in line with the bird as we start our turn. Instinctively we have to decide whether to turn to our left or right (to the left is, of course, easier for right-handers) the turn is executed by the left leg lifting and moving it to a point where we will be finally facing in the opposite direction. To maintain balance and body efficiency, the right heel is raised and swivelling on its ball in the direction of the turn. When the step is completed the weight will be well forward onto the ball of the left foot.

Whilst the turn is being made and when the bird and barrels are well past our neighbours pegs/butts; the left hand starts the process of mounting to the bird. The right hand completes the mount with a tight lock into the cheek simultaneously with the step being completed. The kill picture should be one of the bird being sat well above the bead. To achieve success on the going away birds; always be determined to 'shoot their feet off'.

It will not surprise you that I am going to stress the safety factors here: We never swing the barrels through the line of Guns on a low bird with our guns mounted, always barrels up, stock down. You will do well to practice these movements in stages. Like before, just try the turning. No! You need to turn all the way around so that you are facing the totally opposite direction. Try to keep your left hand in line with the bird as you are turning.

Keep it very simple; remember it is not meant to be a fancy dance step! If you were shooting in front, you would be taking a little walk (one little step) towards your kill position: Now your kill position is immediately behind you, so you are simply going to take a little walk to face there. Yes, your body is going to turn right around; but turning around is a normal body movement. Forget grouse, partridges, guns and shooting for a moment; just practice stepping right around and completing the movement with your weight on your left foot and off your right heel.

Time to bring the clay back into the game; just see it as a bird and point at it as you turn. Good, now pick up the empty gun and practice these movements as though you were going to shoot this bird behind: No! No! You have the gun mounted before the bird and barrels have passed your neighbour's peg. That is 'winging through the line!' Remember: Stock down, barrels up.

OK now you are ready to shoot some. You have not connected yet, but don't get frustrated. You are doing what most other people do at this stage. You are waiting far too long and trying to aim your shot. Your mindset must be to squeeze that trigger as soon as you feel the stock locked in tightly to your cheek. Remember your kill picture should look like shooting the bird's feet:

Try again. Better. You are shooting more quickly, but your shot is passing above the bird because your head is off the stock. This one is a real 'head lifter' an escaping bird (with not much to see on a clay target flying away from you) which you are desperate to succeed on. Don't worry, keep trying, shoot as soon as that stock is locked in, and keep it locked.

Well done; you deserved your reward.

All game shooters would do well to practice this more often during their shooting school sessions.

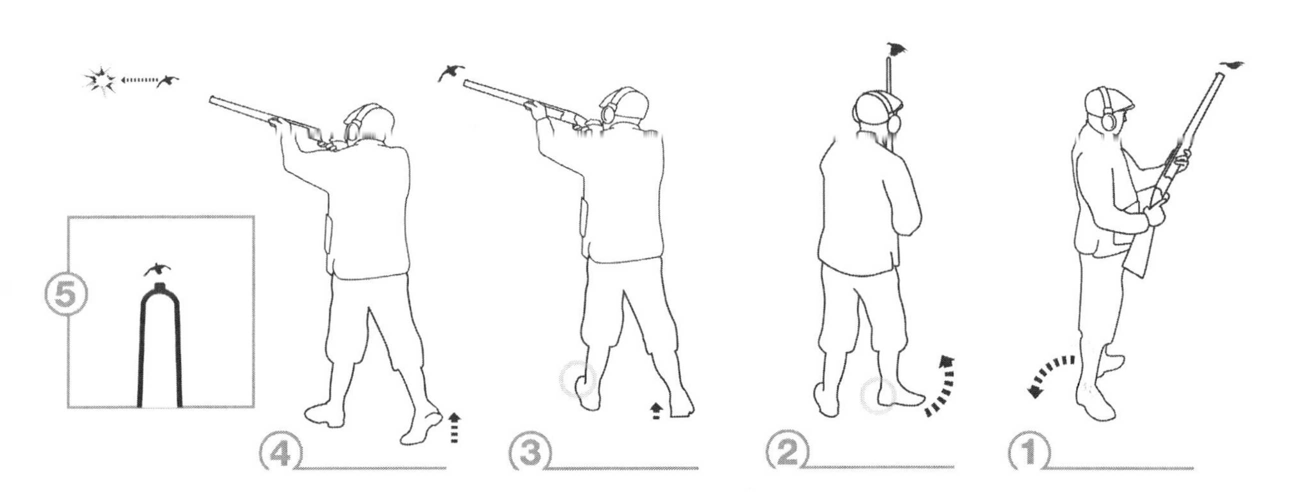

Turning around to shoot a flying away bird

1. *Pick up the bird, left hand remains in contact with the bird's head,barrels raised. Right hand keeps stock well down the body. Left foot lifts and starts to move around (to the left or right)*
2. *Left hand maintains contact with the bird. Right hand keeps the stock down until the barrels have passed the line of neighbouring Guns. Right heel raises, right foot starts to swivel on the ball, following the movement of the left foot.*
3. *Left hand maintains contact with the bird. Weight transfers to the ball of the left foot with right heel raised, body facing kill point.*
4. *Gun is fired when the left hand has made a kill picture that looks like shooting just under the bird (shooting at its feet)*
5. *Shooting at the birds feet*

I am acutely conscious that all diagrams have depicted the use of an *over-and-under* shotgun. This has been solely in an attempt to maintain simplicity and continuity. If each diagram was duplicated with both *over-and-unders* in tandem with *side-by-sides*; I fear the inevitable result would be clutter.

Special Technique for *side-by-side* Users on Rising Crossing Birds

Pupils using *over-and-unders* alongside pupils with *side-by-side*s, receive exactly the same coaching within exactly the same system. There is, however, one aspect of the physical application of using the *side-by-side* that I find myself continually needing to remind the users, that their gun was designed so that the barrels were always placed parallel under the bird. They are reminded that when the bird is driven straight towards or away from them, and they are pointing at it; their barrels will automatically be parallel to it. This will be the case when pointing at the crossing bird flying flat and level. However, it is very common, that when birds are being flushed towards the line of Guns, they are actually climbing. In fact, one of the prime reasons that Guns are stood out as a line in full vision of the approaching birds; is to encourage the birds to lift and make a more challenging and testing shot. When climbing birds pass either side of the Gun using a *side-by-side*, he needs to create a parallel picture. On a bird passing to the left, the right-hander needs to cant (tilt) the barrels to the right just under the bird in order that the angle of the barrels matches exactly the bird's angle of climb. This is the only way to ensure that the gun is moving accurately along the line of the bird's flight.

If the barrels are not kept parallel to the climbing bird; there is a fractional moment when the left hand accelerates to make the kill picture, where the right-hand barrel obscures the bird causing the Gun to lift his head off the stock, resulting in a miss above the bird.

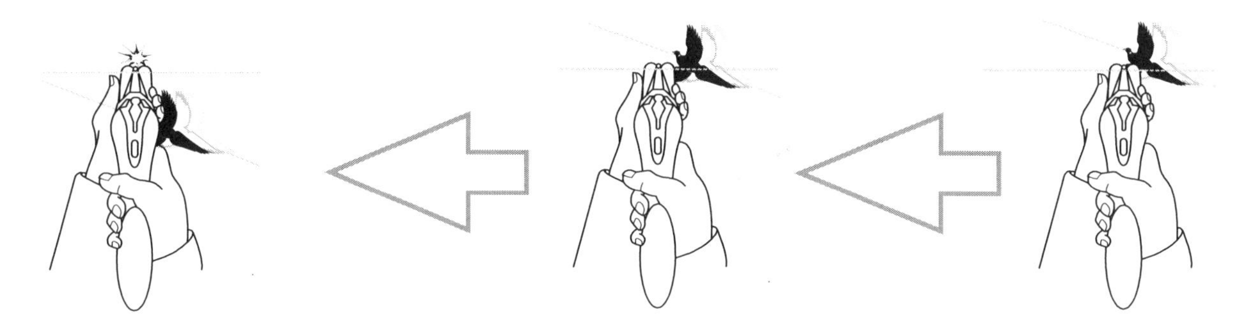

The negative effects of failing to cant the barrels of a side-by-side to keep the barrels parallel with a rising crossing bird

When the climbing bird passes to the right of the right-handed Gun he, of course, cants the barrels to the left to create this parallel picture, ensuring that his left hand barrel does not obscure the bird as it accelerates to make lead. The *over-and-under* user still needs to stay on the line of the bird; but his single narrow sight plane and vertical displacement of the barrels seem to allow this to happen more naturally.

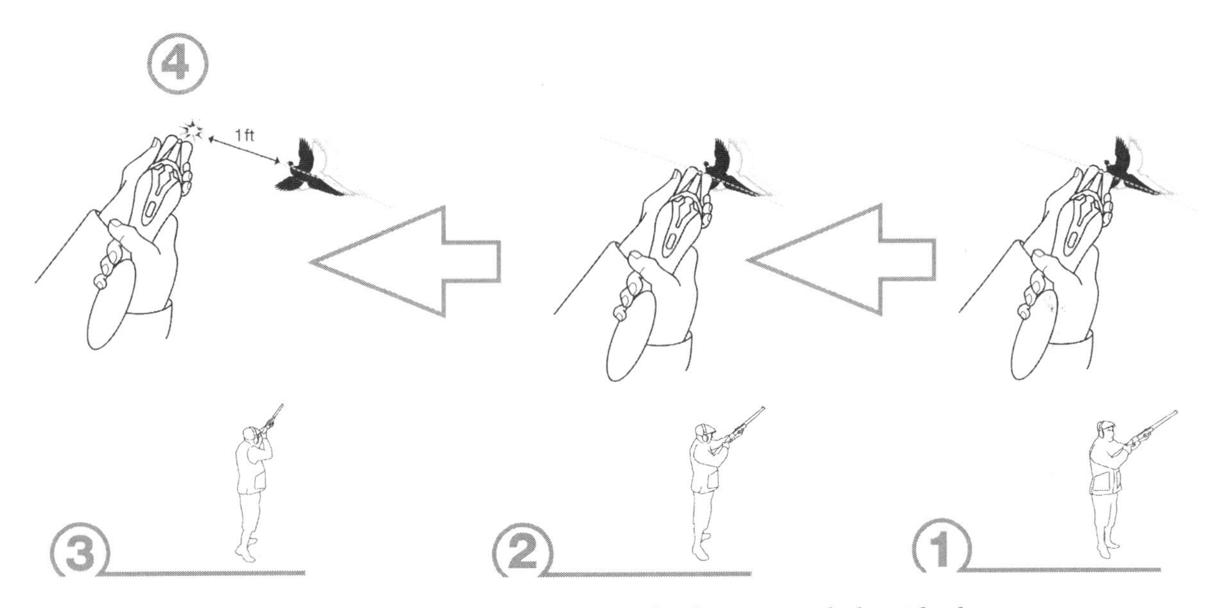

Canting barrels when shooting a rising bird using a side-by-side shotgun

1. *Left hand picks up and cants the barrels to the right (right to left bird). Or.. to the left (left to right bird)*
2. *The left hand keeps the barrels canted to sit under the bird's head and move parallel with the bird*
3. *Right hand locks stock firmly into cheek and shoulder. Left hand pushes barrels ahead to make appropriate kill picture (about 1 foot in front of bird's head). Gun is fired when body and gun are correctly positioned*
4. *Keep barrels parallel with rising flight path of the bird whilst pushing in front.*

Let us take a break from systems and techniques, and look at guns, cartridges, clothing and associated equipment.

Chapter Six
Guns, Clothing & Equipment

Like many of my pupils coming to prepare for game shooting, you already have much of the necessary equipment. However I feel it would be useful for newcomers to compile a list of the essentials that all game shooters should possess.

There can only be one logical item to start with which is of course the shotgun. However, before you can possess that, you have a pre-requisite of two other essential items: a Shotgun Certificate issued by your local constabulary and a suitable secure gun cabinet. Your local police station will provide you with the application form and advise you on its completion, they will also visit the address where your gun will be stored to check and approve your security.

Choice of Gun

Which gun? Well the first decision has to be *side-by-side* or *over-and-under*? A personal choice of course, which may have budgetary influences. An unbiased look at each:

The *side-by-side*: Aesthetically it is very pleasing to the eye (fits many peoples stereotyped idea of how a shotgun should look). It is usually lighter than an *over-and-under* to carry. It is more comfortable to carry broken open in the traditional over the forearm manner and having the chambers *side-by-side* makes for quicker loading.

Disadvantages of the *side-by-side:* The double barrel sight plane is less natural to the eye than a single barrel sight plane of the *over-and-under.* The more common double trigger and straight hand stock requires the hand to move between first and second barrel. The reality of this is that the gun fit is only accurate for one trigger (usually taken from the front one). The slender Fore End provides very little grip and protection from hot barrels. The tendency for *side-by-sides* to be lighter in weight, causes them to inflict recoil discomfort from heavier loads and/or high volume shooting.

The *over-and-under:* The narrow single barrel sight plane leads the eye more naturally. The semi pistol grip and single trigger are more natural and comfortable to hold and lock into the cheek and shoulder. Also, because the hand does not need to move to a second trigger, this makes for better gun fit. The large Fore End that wraps around the barrel makes for more comfortable holding. Heavier weight absorbs recoil better and facilitates use of heavier loads and high volume of shots fired without causing discomfort. The *over-and-under* lends itself well to mass production, making it possible to buy a strong, well-made reliable gun that will withstand heavy use, at an affordable price,

Disadvantages of the *over-and-under*: Rarely as aesthetically pleasing as a Best English Side lock *side-by-side*'. Heavy to carry around. More uncomfortable in the traditional over the forearm hold. Slower to load than a *side-by-side*.

Staying with the 'unbiased' theme; a couple of notes seem appropriate here: Firstly, there are many Best English Sidelock *side-by-side*s that were built with single trigger mechanisms. There are also some Best English *side-by-sides* that were made as much heavier guns suitable to withstand heavier loads and high volume shooting. There are also some extremely attractive looking *over-and-unders*, but they tend to be Best English (both ancient and modern) or at the more expensive end of the mass produced guns. Some of the smaller calibre *over-and-unders* are particularly attractive.

I view the Classic Best English *side-by-side* as a traditional hand-made machine that craftsmen put together utilising their skills amassed over lifetimes. The finished product is a thing of beauty that represents art more than science. The *over-and-under* (other than the few already mentioned) is a mass produced, value-for-money robust, reliable tool designed to be user-friendly and fit for purpose.

To offer a perspective, I shoot game with 12 bore *over-and-unders*. However, when I finally pull off that very large lottery win, a pair of Best English single trigger *side-by-side* sidelocks (two separate actions providing the firing mechanisms one for each barrel. These mechanisms are held in place by side plates often bearing exquisite hand engraving) will be mine! Also, as I write this, if we lined up all of the Guns that had shot game during the past season, the number of *side-by-side*s in use would still outnumber the *over-and-unders*. That ratio has, however, reduced radically during the past 20 years and continues to do so.

Calibre

So, you have decided on your choice of *over-and-under* or *side-by-side*. You may not choose pump actions or semi-automatics for British game shooting. Your next choice is calibre. 12 bores still make up the majority of guns in use on game pegs, but their majority ratio is reducing rapidly, as more and more Guns switch to 20 bores. The efficiency of the modern shotgun cartridge is now understood by more and more game shooters, who have become attracted to the idea of carrying lighter guns and smaller cartridges. The greatest change that I have noticed during the past twenty years, is the move from 12 bore *side-by-sides* to 20 bore *over-and-unders*. I interpret this as a resigned acceptance of the ease of use with an *over-and-under* whilst retaining the lightweight properties of their previously owned *side-by-side*s.

Having chosen your style of gun and calibre, you will have decided on barrel length and chokes. I have no intention of getting into technical opinions about either, however I will suggest that your stature has a logical bearing on the length of barrels that you choose: If you are six foot four, a twenty six inch barrelled gun is hardly going to facilitate smooth gun handling. Conversely, a thirty two inch barrelled gun in the hands of a lightly built five foot tall Gun is hardly going to be the most comfortable and efficient handling choice.

Longer barrels are currently fashionable, but newcomers please let me dispel the myth that longer barrels create a ballistic advantage of sending the shot further. Barrel length is simply a personal choice that provides the most comfortable and efficient gun handling to the individual.

Chokes

Your gun may be fixed choke or multi-choked; although with modern gun engineering, your fixed choke gun can easily be changed to a multi-choked gun. You have to decide if you wish to have the extra versatility of altering the pattern of shot from your gun, by screwing in different sized choke tubes. I have never owned a multi-choked shotgun, but that does not mean that you should not.

The arguments about best choke sizes have been bandied about for as long as I can remember. This is a topic about which I am very happy to sit on the fence. I prefer more open chokes (this my own personal 'simply stack the odds in my favour' wider pattern approach). If I feel that the bird is too high or too far away to result in a clean kill, I don't shoot at it. Yes I have missed plenty of game birds (sometimes more than I am happy to confess to here!) but I honestly believe that none of my misses have been caused by having the wrong chokes in my gun. The next 'expert' that you meet may well dogmatically urge you to use tight chokes to bring down high pheasants, and of course he is entitled to his opinion. You should enjoy experimenting and make your own decisions.

Cartridges

Well, firstly, here is another aspect of your game shooting that you can enjoy experimenting with. I will only make one dogmatic statement; I would urge all game shots to only use biodegradable fibre-wadded cartridges, so that we do not litter the countryside with plastic wads. A growing number of game shooting venues are insisting on a 'fibre wads only' rule.

Modern 'Beretta' game shooting guns. Courtesy of GMK Ltd

I would also like to offer some simple rule of thumb guidelines: Firstly your choice of gun has a bearing; if you are using a light weight *side-by-side*, experiment with loads between twenty five to thirty grams. Should your gun be a heavier *over-and-under*, try out loads between twenty eight and thirty two grams. In both cases, your guns will probably be proofed to take heavier loads, you just need to discover which loads bring in the best results and are most comfortable for you to use.

Your choice of shot size probably alters as you go through the season. My own simple approach is No.7 shot for early season grouse/partridge. No.6 shot for late October/early November pheasants. No.5 shot from December onwards, and my No.5 shot will be a thirty two gram load; occasionally upped to thirty five grams in January or at high bird venues.

Pictures are, of course, much better than words, so it will be much more effective if you can see examples of some of the other ancillary equipment. Firstly, whatever the type of cartridges that you use, you will need a cartridge bag to carry them in. The traditional style with a broad shoulder strap is the most popular. It could be made of leather or canvas, but choose one that holds at least 100 cartridges and buy the best quality that you can afford. I have a leather one which is at least 30 years old, and is still going strong.

Fewer people use them, but you might like to add a cartridge belt to your list. It will add to your carrying capacity, and is a very convenient and comfortable way to carry 25 cartridges around if you are doing a lot of walking. For ease and speed of loading, leather cartridge pouches worn on a separate belt are becoming increasingly popular. They can be worn singly, or one on either side of the body.

Your gun needs cleaning and transporting, so cleaning kits and gun slips are necessary. You are advised to also have a rigid gun case to protect your gun if you are travelling. When you are flying North for the grouse, the airline will insist on your gun being in a locked rigid gun case.

Your comfort and protection

Hearing protection is a must and ear muffs that fit over your ears provide the best long-term protection. You may prefer ear plugs, but I would urge everyone to ensure that children wear ear muffs because their young ears are so easily damaged.

Do consider adding shooting glasses to your kit list. We can never be certain that a stray pellet will not ricochet of an icy hardwood branch and we only have one pair of eyes. These glasses in the right shades will also enhance your vision in various light conditions.

Shooting Clothing

Clothing is an important part of our shooting comfort, but is also a very important part of game shooting's traditional dress code. Whatever style of game shooting clothing that you choose, gentlemen should always wear ties. Historically, game shots have worn hats and ties. Originally this was sensible protection from the weather, as country folk were highly aware of the importance of preventing body warmth being lost through the head and preventing cold reaching the body via the neck area. Hats and ties are now considered the norm in traditional game shooting dress; alongside the knee length breeks (plus twos). These breeks have their origins in comfort and practicality, in that they are much more comfortable than normal long trousers to walk around in all day, particularly on typical grouse moor terrain. On the basis that a game day is a traditional rural social occasion; it is only proper that all Guns and their guests adhere to the dress code.

The breeks might be part of a full shooting suit, which would include a matching waistcoat and overcoat. They may also be worn with a variety of styles of game shooting vests in rustic country colours. All the styles of breeks are worn with knee length stockings, held up with a variety of garters, usually sporting coloured tabs.

Footwear

There is footwear appropriate to your game shooting meeting place. Be it country house, shoot lodge, hotel or pub. The same footwear would also be worn for any of the indoor social aspects of the day. The most traditional form of this indoor footwear would be brown brogues, although other types of smart brown shoes now seem to have become acceptable.

There is now a wide range of suitable outdoor footwear. The main criteria is that they keep your feet warm and dry, whilst being of suitable country shades of green or brown.

This range includes Wellingtons, suitably insulated, boots, sometimes worn with gaiters and calf-length leather boots.

The Ladies (as it, of course, should be) get to choose from a much wider variety of styles of shooting clothing than the men. Long may that continue; they add great fashion, poise, charm and glamour to our game days

(Left) Leather cartridge bag, cartridge belt and gun slip. (Right) Typical modern shotgun cleaning equipment.

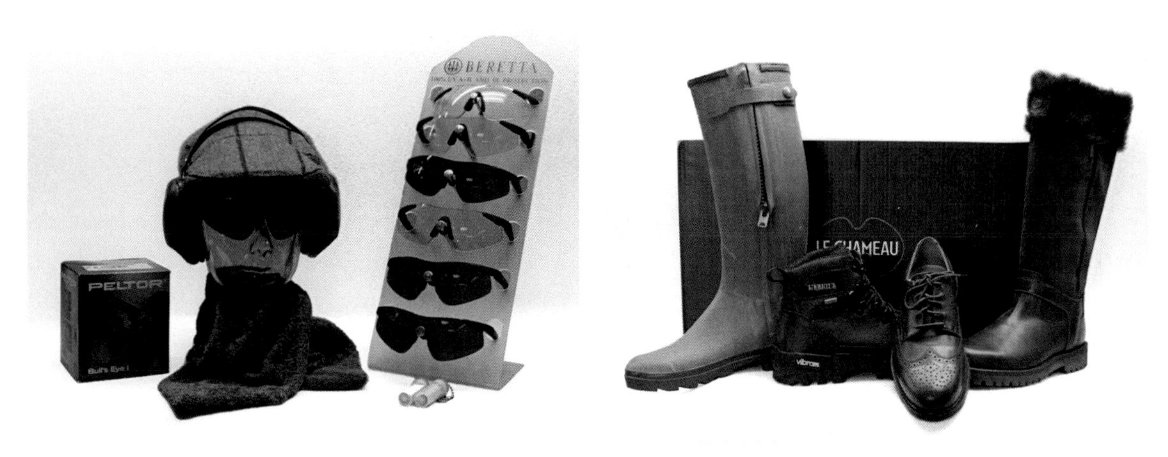

(Left) Protect your eyes and ears. Also keep your your head, neck and throat warm and dry (Right) Modern gameshooting footwear

Everyone, regardless of gender, has at least one waterproof topcoat, most of which contain Gortex or similar breathable material. A ‘pull over’ pair of some type of waterproof over trousers generally completes the game shooters wet weather kit. It is now extremely rare to see anyone wearing the waxed type of waterproof coat.

A selection of fashionable modern game shooting clothing from the expansive Alan Paine range

A happy team of lady guns dressed; warmly, traditionally, fashionably & attractively on a very cold, frosty day

Other optional equipment

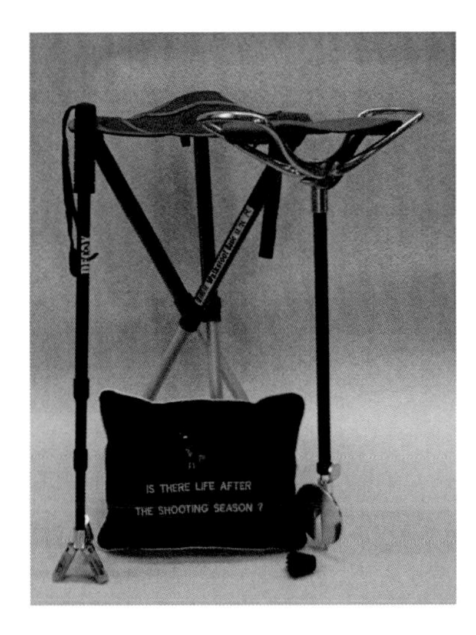

Magnet & shooting seats.

All accessories supplied by, and photographed at 'Wiltshire Rod & Gun', Swindon.

You might like to add a shooting stick to your list of 'must haves'. This could be one that acts as a walking stick, with a fold down leather or metal seat, a very useful addition on sloping and/or slippery terrain. It may even have a magnet at one end to aid the collection of spent cartridge cases. You can have a magnet which is not part of a seat stick, which can be clipped to your belt, cartridge bag or gunslip. It can have a weighted end and be used as a **priest** (an implement used to dispatch a wounded bird quickly). This could also be a weighted piece of bone, antler or wood. There are also folding three legged stools with leather seats, carried on a strap over the shoulder. Not quite so practical as the seat walking stick, but more comfortable and stable.

You might choose to pause here and remind yourselves what a great favour you have bestowed on your families and friends, as you have provided them with such a comprehensive list of suitable future Christmas, Birthday and anniversary presents!

Insurance

When looking at everything that you should possess for game shooting, there is one more essential item that all game shots must be in possession of: PUBLIC LIABILITY INSURANCE. Not to have it is irresponsible! You can easily organize it through your own broker but your own, and game shooting's, best interests will be best served if you arrange your insurance through one of the shooting bodies such as those detailed here:

The Countryside Alliance, The Old Town Hall,
367 Kennington Road, London, SE11 4PT.
0207 840 9200
www.countryside-alliance.org

The Countryside Alliance (CA) is the only organisation to actively champion country life and defend the liberties of the people who live and work there. They describe their vision as being one that sees a vital, working and thriving countryside that benefits everyone. The CA campaigns vigorously to change public and political attitudes towards shooting. Their campaigning activities are based on extensive research into the reasons why the public will support shooting. In addition to their campaign work, the CA has a membership system - benefits include £10 million Public Liability insurance for all recognised Field Sports activities.

The British Association for Shooting And Conservation.
Marford Mill, Rossett, Wrexham,
LL12 0HL
01244 573000
www.basc.org.uk

The BASC is the UK's largest shooting organisation that currently has 130,000 members. As a National representative body for Sporting shooting, it has five strategic objectives:

- A strong and unified voice for shooting.
- All party backing for shooting.
- Balanced comment in the media.
- Continued opportunity to go shooting.
- Maintaining the highest of standards in sporting shooting.

BASC describes its mission as promoting and protecting sporting shooting and the well-being of the countryside throughout the UK and overseas. They protect their members' interests by providing a voice for sporting shooting (which includes wildfowling, game shooting and rough shooting, deer stalking, pigeon shooting, pest control, air gunning and gun dogs). BASC also promotes practical habitat conservation and the setting of standards. It is continually involved in the undertaking of appropriate research projects.

Chapter Seven
High pheasants - Shooting With a Neighbour

During this lesson, we are going to get to grips with mastering the high pheasant challenges. Before we look at the techniques, it seems appropriate to clarify what I mean by '**high pheasants**'. I am describing birds flying at 100 to 120 feet. However there will be many very experienced Guns, who do not consider the bird to be truly high until it is at 150 feet. We are now into the subject matter, but I believe that any Gun who consistently achieves clean kills on birds at 100 feet, is shooting very well indeed.

Achieving consistent success on high pheasants would be most game shooters' ultimate satisfaction. If that consistency included regular rights-and-lefts, that would surely be the icing on the cake. There may be others who would consider that their ultimate game shooting buzz was consistently achieving a right-and-left out of every covey of partridges that flew over them. Who would argue that taking two birds out of a covey of grouse in front of the butt, reloading (or of course receiving your second gun from your loader) turning and taking two more birds out of the same covey, might give you a very special high?

Back to reality, and the high pheasant. Why should this particular shot be so satisfying? Because it is so difficult. The mechanics of this shot are not particularly difficult, however the psychological factors are. The high pheasant is just another moving target, so why is it the *Achilles heel* for so many game shooters? I must assume that it is the especially strong desire to succeed on this particular shot that creates those psychological barriers that cause so many misses. I have already put it on record, that word I use the most at the shooting school is 'lock'. The words most commonly hear from my pupils are 'If only I could shoot consistently well on those high pheasants!'

So what is the secret of success? The simple truthful answer is timing and lock. Breaking that down, let us look at the timing. Remember that I commented, that it was because we are so keen to succeed that we create problems, and one of the most common problems that we create is mounting the gun far too soon (getting too excited). The stock is locked into the cheek far too early along the birds flight path.

When we looked at shooting the driven pheasant at 60/70 feet, I suggested that the best kill point was at about seventy to eighty degrees; and I would encourage you to carry on doing that. However, on the high driven pheasants, I am going to suggest that you change to a kill point that is 80/90 degrees, and here is my reasoning: Waiting until the bird is almost overhead brings it as close as it is going to be. Also most of the bird is exposed at this angle, making it most vulnerable. If you are using your body, as I have suggested, with your weight through the ball of your front foot and rear heel raised, you will be very supple at the waist and will be able to move your torso very efficiently.

Now to the lock. When we mount the gun too soon, we are tracking the bird for too long with a fully mounted gun; in effect we have turned the shotgun into a rifle, and try to 'aim our lead'. This translates into conscious thought processes and mechanical movements that are striving for precision. In really simple terms, we are just 'trying too hard' which invariably results in a brief hesitation with the head lifted off the stock.

Learning and Practicing the Technique

Enough theory; let us get into the practical application. Firstly, get the eyes, brain, body, hands and feet loosened up with the ordinary bird. Load up, shoot a few. Point, shut, step, lock, push. No problems at all. Now the higher one. This is a midi clay driven over you at about 100 feet. Perfect size, remember you are going to see it as a pheasant's head. Watch a few in flight and mentally rehearse your timing; fix a spot above you where you are going to be killing it, you have lots of time, and you are going to be slowing down your gun mount. Your lock must happen later than it did on the lower Driven bird.

Try a few with an empty gun - same sequence: Point, shut, step, lock very tight, and push hard.

You need to slow down the mount, be content to keep that stock away from your face as you slowly take the barrels towards the bird. Try a few shots. No luck yet? You need to push the barrels harder (get them further in front) with much more aggression in your left hand. You need to have your barrels about 4 feet in front of this bird. OK you have killed a couple, but because you are shooting with one eye shut, you cannot see your kill picture (lead) so blind faith is required! This is where the 'one eye shut' Gun becomes penalised. So how about we level the playing field?

You have just become a member of 'the 50% club'. I reckon that about 50% of Guns who shoot high pheasants, struggle to cope with them if they try to take them as straight on Driven birds when they are shooting with one eye shut; so they create a simple solution, by turning the Driven bird into a crossing bird. You can do the same: Remember the footwork you learned for the crossing bird. You are going to use that to turn your body ninety degrees. Of course you have to make an instant decision about whether you are going to turn to your left or right. For this exercise, step to your right, this will make the high bird a left-to-right crosser where it will need the most lead and the tightest lock, and being the more difficult bird, will give you the best practice scenario.

Shoot this bird when it is crossing you at ninety degrees to your right, but remember it will also be up above you. You need to see a kill picture (lead) that looks like missing it about 6 feet in front. Off you go, try a few. Slow down, mount the gun more slowly, (lock later). OK a couple of tips: Having the bird right above you can make you feel a little uncomfortable and off balance, so don't be shy about stepping a few paces backwards after you have turned ninety degrees. Also, you need to turn your barrels ninety degrees and stay just under the bird (*over-and-unders* turning ninety degrees and staying vertical under the bird, *side-by-side*s turning ninety degrees and staying parallel under the bird).

Have another attempt. You need to lock much tighter, and make a bigger kill picture. When you feel that you have taken the barrels too far in front of that bird, squeeze the trigger! Well done! I am sure that you were convinced that you were going to miss a long way in front. You now know that you can do it. You just have to practice enough so that you believe that you will do it! Remember: High birds need good timing and plenty of lock.

Do practice these high birds as much as you can, and vary your turning so that you are stepping both to your left and to your right. When you are feeling more confident, walk forward a few paces at a time. Walking forward will increase the relative crossing rate of the clay target flying over you, until you reach a point where it will be passing over you as fast as any pheasant can fly. Also walk across the clay's line of flight, in both directions, so that you can experiment with assessing and changing the kill picture (lead) for high birds at different angles and distances.

Those Guns that get to be under high pheasants on a regular basis are usually the ones that perform best. However, anyone who is prepared to practice as often as possible with the exercises that I have described, will be stacking the odds in their favour. Building a library of kill pictures for the high birds will give you the best chance to succeed when you finally find yourself underneath them.

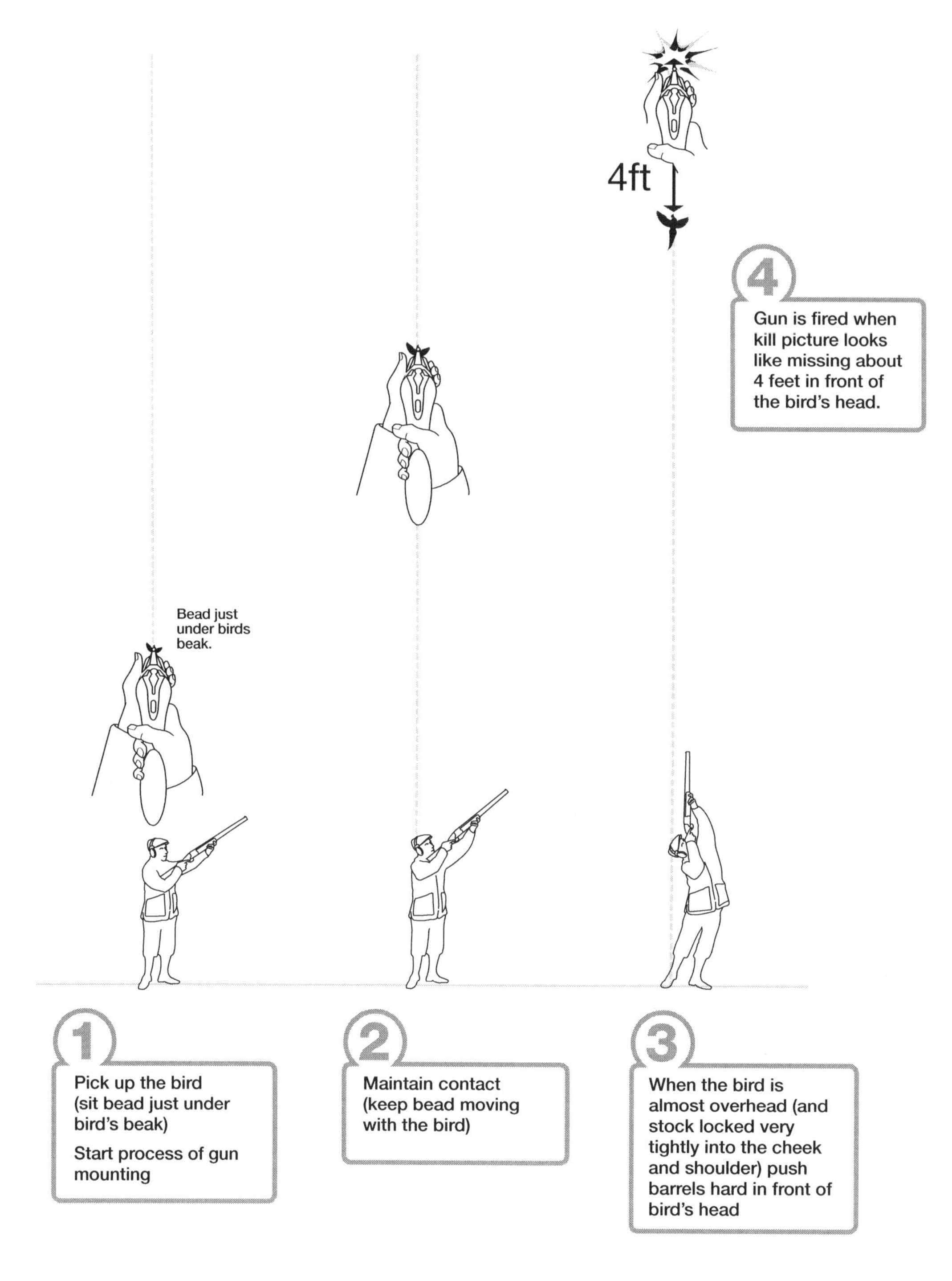

Shooting a high Driven bird with both eyes open

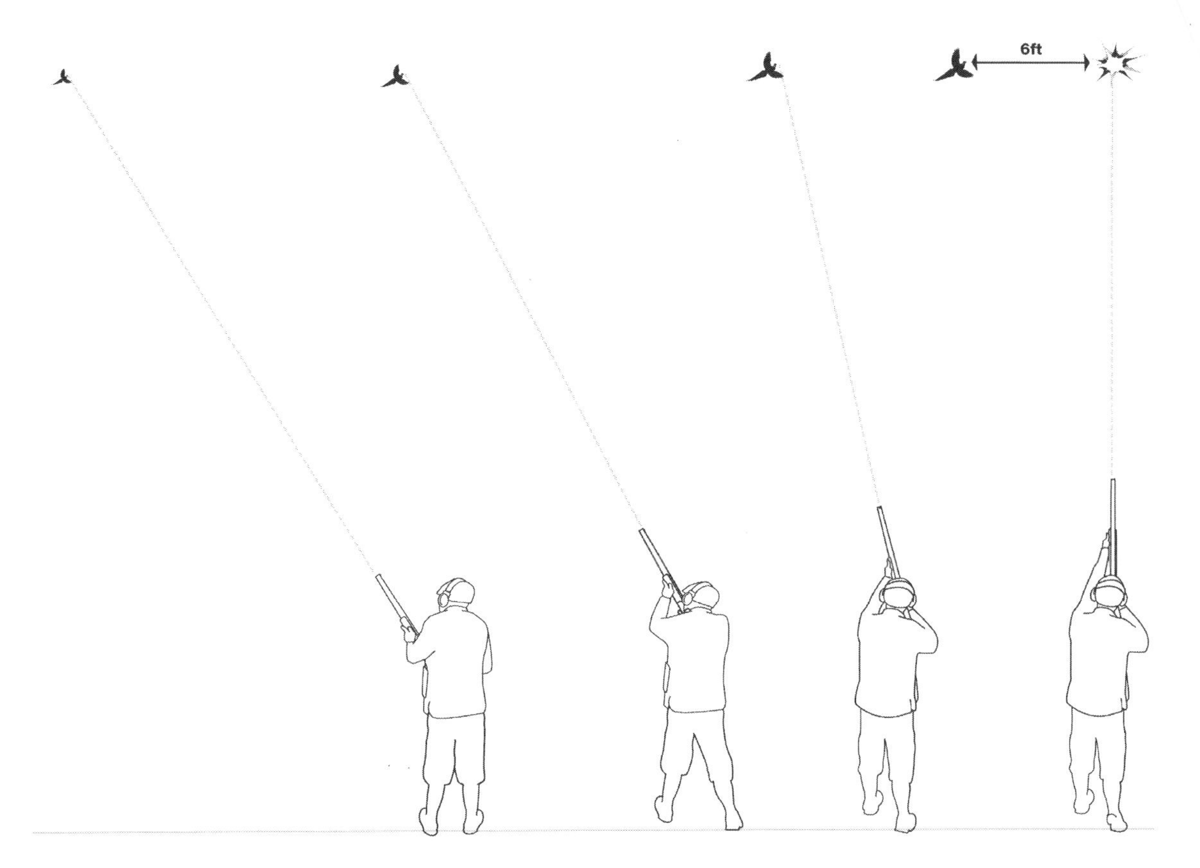

Shooting a high, left-to-right crossing bird. The high right to left crossing bird needs a kill picture that looks like missing the front of the bird's head by about 6 feet. n.b. Lead (kill picture distances) will need to be adjusted to match the height and distance of the bird.

An Alternative Approach to Tackling the High Driven Pheasant When Shooting with One Eye Shut

Before we move on to shooting with a neighbour, I would like to offer just one more system to the 50% of 'one eye shut' Guns who struggle with the high Driven bird. Some Guns in this group just cannot cope with the very strong mental objection of deliberately obscuring (blotting out) the bird. Remember this has got nothing to do with ability, it is just the way an individual's brain works. This same group may not like turning to make the bird into a 'crosser' as they very strongly believe that they should be able to take the bird 'driven' as it was presented. If you fit into this category, here is something for you to try:

You will need to go back to your shooting school, and must be prepared to experiment and practice. Get the coach to present you with an average driven clay, just like we started with in our first session. Now the radical (but very simple bit). Instead of pointing at it, point a little bit to the right of it (opposite for left-handers). Push in front, see the lead and fire. Don't be surprised when it disappears in a puff of dust. Just shoot some more, then move onto a higher bird when you must point a little further to the right of it. When you are killing that one consistently, move onto the 100 foot bird. Point about 1 foot to the right and push to make a kill picture that looks like you are pointing about 4 feet in front of it. Again do not be surprised when you kill it, just keep practising (including shooting at Driven birds presented randomly at varying heights.)

Within 30 minutes, you will know if you like this system or not; however it is only going to work for you if you practice it. When you are taking these practice shots at birds of varying heights and moving your barrels further away (or closer) to the driven clay target, mentally rehearse pictures of your barrels moving different distances along the bird's wing . These pictures are, of course, what you are going to need to make and recognise on the actual driven pheasants. When the next high driven pheasant flies straight towards you, sit the end of its left wing tip just above you gun barrel bead - push until it looks like you are going to miss about 4 feet in front and fire. If you keep your head locked tight, I promise you that you will be a 'happy Gun'.

You will logically ask how this works. I am simply going to tell you that because you can see what you are doing, you will succeed and the pattern will do the rest: you just need to try it then believe it.

Shooting With Neighbours

To date, during coaching sessions, you have been shooting as an individual. However to best prepare you for your first day out, you are going to be shooting the clays as though you have neighbours either side of you. Initially your neighbours will be imaginary whilst you learn which birds are yours and which are your neighbours'.

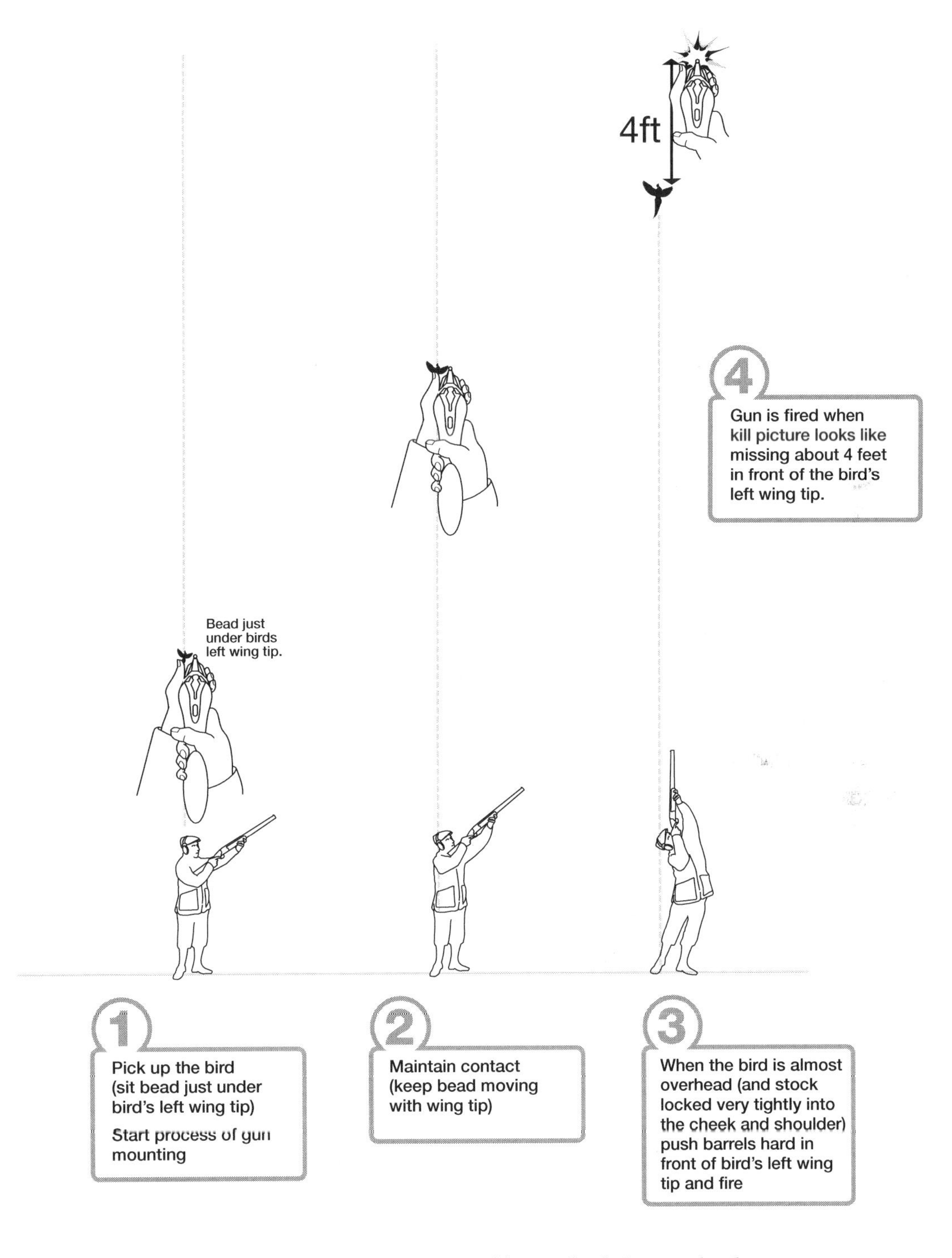

A one eyed shut shooter tackling a high Driven bird.

I have placed that black tub about 30 yards to your left (30 to 40 yards is a typical distance between pegs). Now I am going to throw a random sequence of clays from six different clay traps towards you. Before I start, look to both sides of you and draw an imaginary line half way between where you are and where your neighbours would be. When I start sending the clays, just point at those that you think are inside your imaginary lines (closer to you than your neighbours). To add a little additional realism, I have set one of the traps to present you with a clay target which is set at a height which I believe is too low to represent a sporting pheasant. Let me show it to you, here it is. Whenever this one appears, just ignore it.

For this exercise, just point at the clays that you believe represent sporting birds that are yours. Off we go, pretty simple really. OK now do the same exercise but pointing an empty gun. Good, still pretty simple. Now shoot some. Not quite so straight forward now is it? Birds are flying, you have a loaded gun; and quite naturally you want to shoot them. This is your preparation for the 'real' thing. You now have to have a completely new and different mind-set. From now on, it is all about you shooting the clays (remember they represent birds) that are safe, sporting and yours!'

Have another go. Good, you did not shoot any low ones, and only shot a couple of your neighbours' birds.

Time for even more realism: You will now have an actual neighbour who will be shooting from the peg to your left; here he is on his way to the peg. He is loading up, you do the same: Last reminder; be very conscious about keeping your barrels up at a safe angle at all times. The drive has started, here come the birds! Not so easy to be disciplined now you are actually shooting is it? When the birds appear, some of them may well seem to be in your arc, and they may actually be at the start of their flight, but if you watch them carefully, you will see that they are actually flying into your neighbours' arcs. The deciding criteria is which Gun is the bird flying towards? Should you shoot a bird that is in your arc in the early stages of its flight, but is actually flying towards one of your neighbours; the embarrassing result may well be a dead pheasant landing at your neighbour's feet: Very bad form!

Try again; think carefully about which birds that you are going to shoot and take your time. That is very good. Unload and swap places with your neighbour so that you get to shoot at different birds.

Load up and start again. Now the birds coming to you are being shot just as you are going to shoot them. Every time you are about to squeeze the trigger, the clay that you have locked on to shatters! This is very frustrating for you; even though these are just clay birds that your neighbour is shooting.

I actually asked him to do that. I told him that I wanted you to experience how it felt to have a Greedy Gun as a neighbour. Hopefully you will never actually have that experience when you are on a game peg, because as you discovered, it is very frustrating and off-putting. Greedy Guns rarely receive a second invitation!

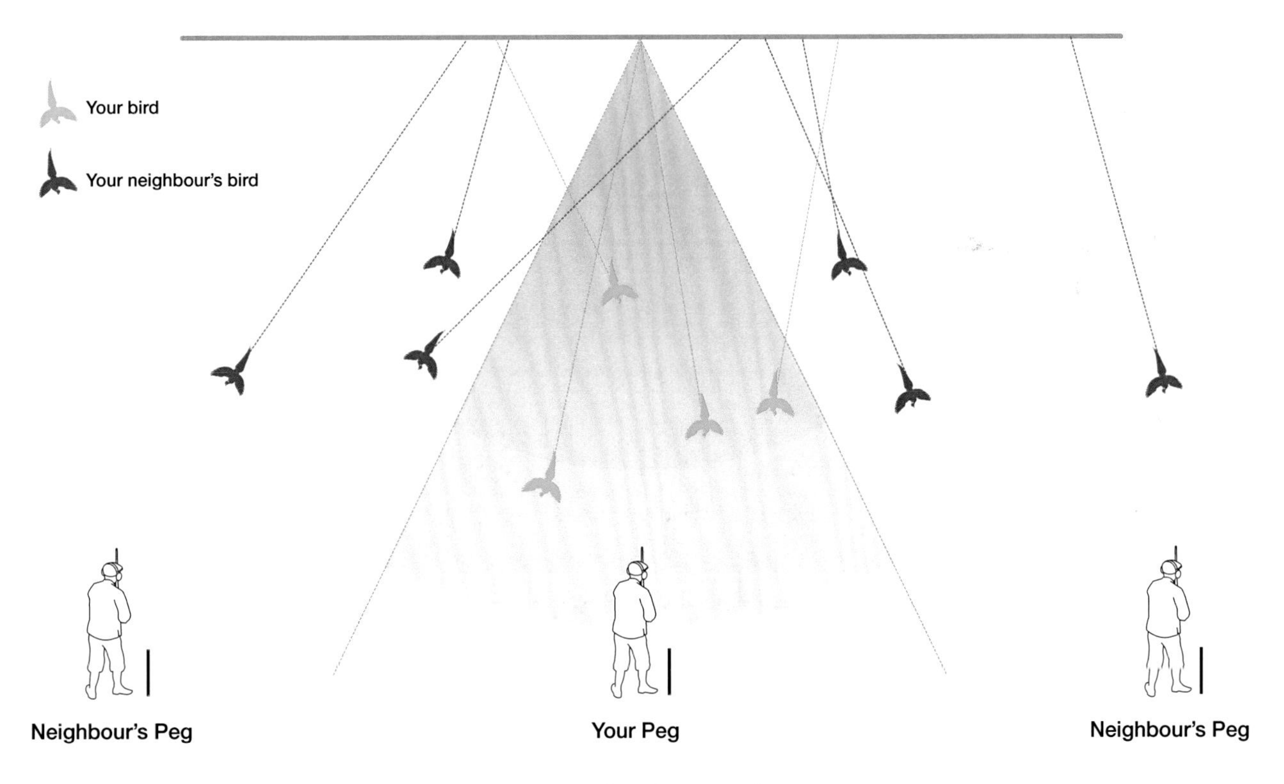

The correct etiquette for shooting from game pegs.

N.B. Low Birds.

It is extremely difficult to give a finite description of what actually constitutes a low bird. When I am stood with novices in the field, I actually encourage them to shoot at birds (providing that I am sure that they are 100% safe) that I would not expect a more experienced Gun to shoot at. However, once they have connected with a few, and are feeling more confident, I give them some simple guide-lines:

- If you feel that you cannot miss, it is too low/close
- If you can see its eyes it is too low/close
- When there is more than one bird flying in your arc, shoot the highest/ most challenging one.

When you are the **flank** (end of line) Gun and a January cock pheasant flies out to your side six feet above the ground forty yards distant, you have a very sporting testing shot (with the usual safety checks). As you become more experienced and competent; you will become more selective and discerning about the birds that you are happy to shoot.

You are now very aware of all the aspects of game shooting that you need to practice. However, before I take you out for your first game day; I would like to give you an insight and good understanding of all the hard work that goes on behind the scenes.

When I have explained the planning and effort that takes place during the gamekeeper's year to produce the game day that you are going to attend, I am sure you will value your enjoyment of the experience even more.

Chapter Eight
Behind the Scenes

I always try to give all newcomers as much background information as is practicable. In my experience, the more people understand what goes on behind the scenes, the more they enjoy their new pastime.

Whenever possible, I take my pupils to view a release pen as I believe that this is the best starting point for the newcomer to begin to understand the basic strategy and layout of modern game shoots.

The Release Pen

To date, my most effective descriptive analogy appears to be when I liken the release pen to a budgerigar cage, but on a massive scale. The birds in the cage will be supplied with food and water. The food will be supplied in such a way that the birds can spend time enjoying pecking away at it. Most cages will contain bells, ladders, and mirrors to keep the birds amused. Cages will be supported on a high stand, out of the reach of cats and dogs. The mesh of the cage is designed so that it prevents the entry of pets' paws and curious children's hands. The cage will be roomy enough for the birds to move around in freely, with a door that has a very secure fastening system to keep the birds safely inside.

Before the birds are let out of the cage to enjoy some flying time, pets are shut out of the room that has all windows firmly shut.

(Left) An essential water supply for the game birds. (Right) Modern feed hoppers alongside a maize game crop that has been planted strategically close to woodland.

Now to the release pen. It is roomy enough to allow the pheasant poults a healthy amount of comfortable space to co-exist in. Hoppers provide food that drops onto straw that the birds love to scratch around in. Drinkers provide a constant supply of fresh clean water. Whilst there will not be bells, ladders and mirrors, there will be piles of branches, logs, dusting shelters and straw to climb on and scratch around in and under. There will also be bushes and trees of varying heights to provide roosting for the birds as they learn to fly up to roost. Most importantly, the mesh of the pen will be of sufficient strength and height to keep predators out. There will be an electric fence around the perimeter to add to the birds' security. The best release pens have sufficient foliage to provide warmth and shelter in inclement weather, plus shade for the hottest days and open sunny areas for the pheasants to enjoy basking in.

The budgerigar owner bought his cage at a pet store; the gamekeeper did not buy his, he built it with his own hands. Many keepers now work single handedly, so the pen building and many other jobs in the keeper's year require the help of his network of friends that he has carefully built up over the years. This network will almost always include neighbouring gamekeepers and it will also include other key people that can provide a variety of different skills.

In my attempts to help newcomers understand the strategic siting of release pens, game strips, cover crops and coverts, I use a picture of a cartwheel as a simple descriptive analogy. I describe the hub of the wheel as the location of the release pen, the spokes going out from the hub are game strips and/or hedgerows leading to the holding and flushing areas of coverts/cover crops, which are sited along the rim of the cartwheel.

(Left) The Gamekeeper checking the wire of a release pen. (Right) The electric fence at the perimeter of a release pen used as an added defence against four legged predators.

During a game day, the Guns see the gamekeeper as the person (there are a few female gamekeepers) marshalling and organizing the beating team in its role of flushing and presenting sporting birds over the Gun line. Rarely do they ever get to see and understand the multitude of activities that have taken place 'behind the scenes'.

The Gamekeeper's Year

As far as the Guns are concerned, the main game shooting season ends on 1st February. Gamekeepers may well believe that their season actually starts on 2nd February - a very busy programme commences here. Starting in February, the keeper (and hopefully a couple of key helpers) **catch-up** (collect) hen pheasants. This is a very physical process that takes place early in the morning and then again in the evening at around dusk. These birds will be the egg-laying stock for the coming season and, depending on the size of the shoot, the keeper may have to catch up many hundreds of them.

If the shoot does not have a permanent aviary, or possibly a number of aviaries (many do not), an aviary has to be built by the keeper. The same predator security provided at the release pen is required for the aviary with the addition of a net that must cover the top of it. These aviaries of course need **feed hoppers**, (variously shaped drums that facilitate birds pecking and dropping feed onto straw) which require regular topping up, in tandem with a constant fresh water supply. In heavy frosts, automatic running water supplies may freeze up, so water must then be carried to the aviaries by hand.

The caught up hens are put into the aviaries accompanied by a number of cock pheasants, that replicates the ratios of cock to 'harem of hens' that would take place in a natural wild state. Depending on numbers and successes, catching-up may continue into March.

Alongside the dawn and dusk catching-up activities, there are many other tasks that will ensure that the keeper is kept busy. The daily setting and checking of tunnel traps is essential and very time consuming. It is critical to control the numbers of the smaller four legged predators before the egg-laying begins. The maize game crop areas need the remaining stalks to be chopped down so that the ground can be ploughed, fertilized and prepared for re-planting. New areas of land may also need to be prepared as new sites for game crops.

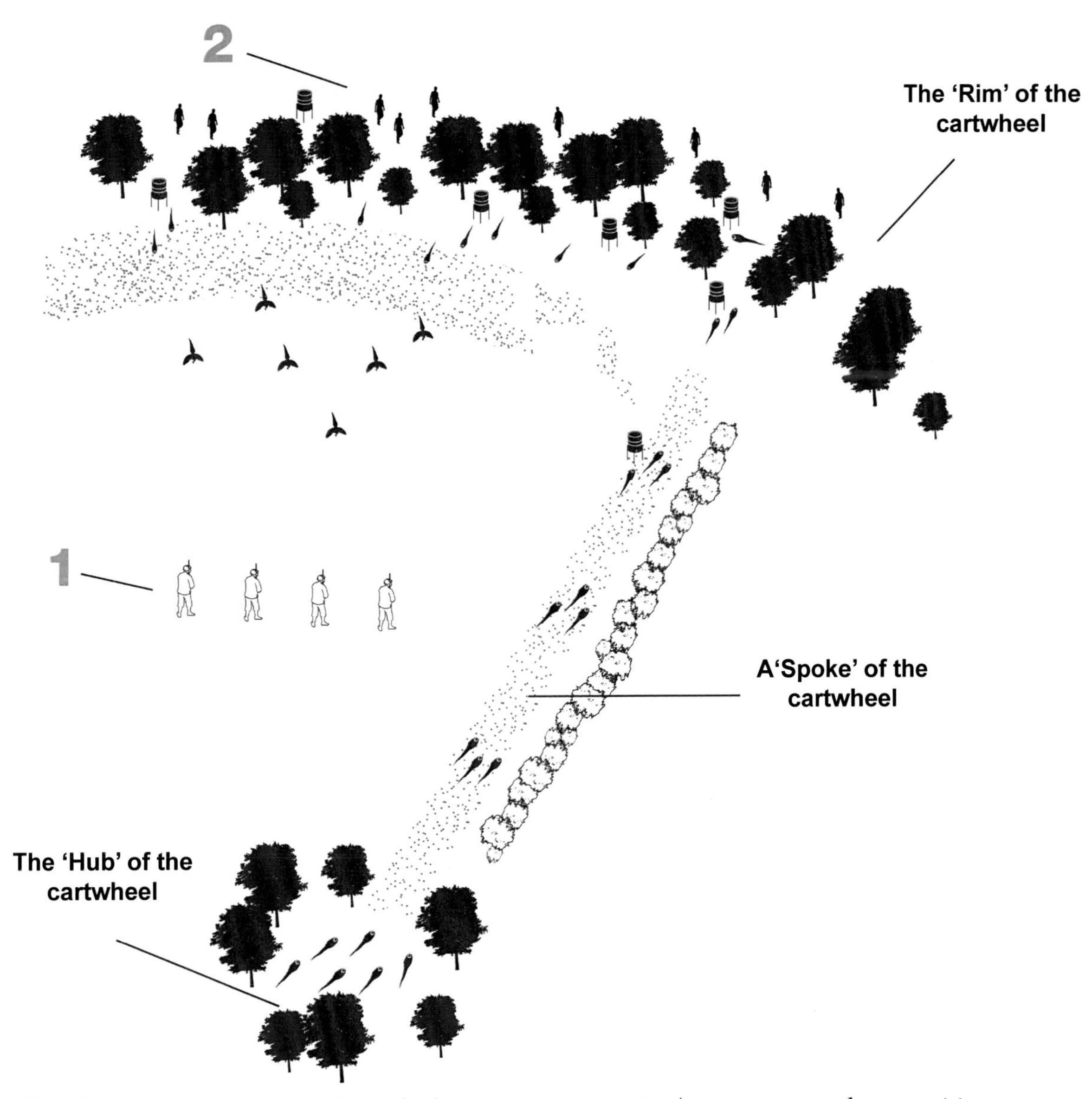

The "Cartwheel" strategic siting of release pen, game strips/cover crops and peg positions.

*The '**Hub**' of the 'Cartwheel' - The Pheasant release pen situated in woodland.*
*A '**Spoke**' of the 'Cartwheel' - Game strip and hedgerow providing a safe and convenient route for the pheasants to walk to a 'Covert' (wood) for food and shelter.*
*The '**Rim**' of the 'Cartwheel - A 'Covert' and Flushing game crop.*

1. *Strategic siting of the line of pegs to place the Guns between flushing Game crop and release pen*
2. *Beaters walk the pheasants into the Game crop, then through the crop until the birds 'Flush' over the Guns*

At least two Saturdays in February will see the gamekeeper fully occupied. His first Saturday is when he organizes and runs the traditional hare shoot day. This is when his beaters, picking-up team and key helpers, all turn out with their shotguns to walk the shoot ensuring that hare population numbers are kept at manageable levels. This event requires very careful management and marshalling. The second Saturday is taken up as a vermin day: Another shooting day out for the keepers' team, and one that is very important in the shoot's calendar as an additional method of reducing the amount of vermin that will be attracted to game birds' eggs. To the untrained casual eye, this may just look like a group enjoying a wander through the woods taking the odd pot shot. The reality is that it takes careful planning and strategic positioning of the walking Guns if there is to be any chance of outwitting the wily cunning of the crows, magpies and jays.

During March, the catching-up of hens continues, as does the continued siting and checking of tunnel traps. Any spare daylight hours are taken up with all necessary forestry work, replanting ground cover in the coverts, replanting/repairing hedgerows, planting new coverts and planting evergreen screens. Alongside these tasks, time must be found for the essential culling of the deer (doe) population which create an ever increasing amount of damage throughout the countryside.

(Left) A tunnel trap. One of the control methods of smaller four-legged predators.
(Right) A Larsen trap. Used as part of the control of Corvid predators.

After dark, the keeper and key helpers will be out with shotguns **lamping for rabbits** (this involves an extra powerful large torch that projects a very powerful beam of light to facilitate night-time shooting) for rabbits. This will continue until the cereal crops have grown. Lamping for the foxes with a rifle is another essential night-time task for the keeper. He needs to control the rabbit population to protect his game crop and forestry planting. However this control is also essential to protect all the other crops that provide income to the estate/farm. Likewise for fox control, the keeper's first priority is to protect his game bird population from this particular predator. In doing this, he also provides critical protection for any lambs and/or fowl that are part of the commercial operation of the estate/farm.

Should the gamekeeper want to take his family on holiday, he will need to arrange it so that it takes place during this month. However, to achieve this he will need to organise his friends/key people to carry out all the essential March tasks. Whoever is covering for him, will also have to allocate time to feed and exercise the keeper's dogs - and there may well be half a dozen of those.

During April, the keeper will need to allocate some of his time acting as a deer guide to clients of the estate who wish to shoot bucks as part of the annual deer cull. Whilst this is very time-consuming for the keeper, it is an important source of extra revenue for the estate. **Tunnel trapping** (an effective method of controlling small, four-legged predators), rabbit and fox control also continue throughout this month. Any release pens that need repairing and/or re-siting become additional daylight tasks. There may also be new pens to be built in other areas of the shoot. **Larsen traps** (an effective method of controlling winged predators) for magpies and crows are also built and sited at this time of year, and they will be checked at least twice daily. As April progresses, the hen pheasants begin laying; so now the aviaries need to be visited two or three times a day to check for, and collect eggs which need to be washed.

May sees the busy game crop planting begin, which can extend into June depending on the weather conditions and type of game crops being planted. Partridge and pheasants eggs are now being set in the incubators. Between these tasks, the keeper finds time to set up the rearing fields to take the chicks when they are mature enough to leave the incubating sheds.

During June the first hatch of chicks should be ready to be moved to the rearing fields. Aviaries that were temporary structures will be dismantled and stored away. Final touches and inspections are given to all the release pens, because, at the very end of the month, they need to be ready to house the young pheasant poults.

July is the busiest month for releasing the young poults into the pens and is a critical time for the well-being of the young birds; when they are most susceptible to inclement weather, disease and predators. The keeper will be keeping a very watchful eye on all his release pens ensuring that his birds have ample feed in the hoppers and water in the drinkers.

During August, partridge pens will be sited ready to receive the young birds that will be released in September.

September is a very busy month. Hoppers are now sited in the woods as the young pheasants have found their way to them via the maize cover strips. The rearing fields and equipment are all cleared away with everything disinfected before it is put into store.

One of the most time consuming tasks and a constant headache is **dogging-in** (using dogs to keep the pheasants within desired areas). Now that the cereal crops have been harvested there is ample natural food in the stubble fields and from the variety of hedgerows berries. It is now virtually impossible to prevent the young pheasants from wandering around freely. To ensure that these young birds are kept within the areas that the keeper wants them, he (hopefully with a couple of helpers) will spend many hours out with their dogs walking the birds back to designated locations. This may need to be done two or three times a day.

The stubble fields will allow a return to night-time lamping to resume control of the rabbit and fox population. The young pheasants are particularly vulnerable to the fox; who is often lying hidden waiting to pounce when the young birds drop down to the ground from roosting at 'first light'. The partridge season has officially started on the first day of this month; so some keepers are already involved in running their shoot days.

October is generally seen as the month that the game shooting season starts in earnest. The partridge shooting is in full swing, and those shoots that released their pheasants early enough, have mature birds ready to shoot by the middle of the month. Gamekeepers, beaters and picking-up teams are now fully engaged with the game shooting season. Beaters and picking-up teams will be working on a number of different shoots. In some parts of the country, that could involve them being out six days a week. When the gamekeepers are not running their own days, they are probably helping out on neighbouring shoots; however, their own birds still need feeding, watering and protecting, seven days a week.

When you stand on your peg for the first drive of the day; and a magnificent cock pheasant breaks cover and climbs higher and higher as it speeds towards the line of Guns, you can now appreciate the amount of effort that was put in to get it there. There are many people combining their skills behind the scenes, but it is the gamekeeper who is the hinge pin of it all. I wonder what the perfect CV of a gamekeeper would list as essential qualifications and experiences

The Gamekeeper's C.V.

Ornithologist. He must understand birds; certainly game birds and winged predators.

Farmer. He will always be liaising with an estate/farm Manager, and must understand the workings and demands of the agricultural year. He also needs to be able to be proficient with much of the farming machinery, particularly the tractor and all of its associated equipment.

Agronomist. He better have a good understanding of the soil and the game crops that he sows, for they are essential throughout the shooting part of his season.

Forester . He will need to know how to care for shrubs, hedgerows and trees.

Veterinary Assistant. He will not be expected to be the local vet, but he will need to recognize when his birds are diseased and how to care for them. He will also need a good knowledge of dog husbandry.

Dog Trainer. The dogs are an essential part of the keepers life; he will need to be able to train different types of dogs for different roles.

Carpenter and Mechanic. The keeper continually has a requirement to build or repair something out of wood, he also needs to be able to give at least basic maintenance to the variety of tools and equipment that he uses.

Manager and Leader. Those beaters and helpers are not in attendance because of high salaries. They are there because they want to be, and they want to give their best to the keeper, who has the task of getting them to work as an efficient team. Which they must do willingly and happily.

Diplomat and Ambassador. When Mrs. Jones has just let her pet poodle run through the cover crop of maize that was holding the pheasants for the first drive; he somehow needs to muster an appropriate amount of diplomacy. On a shoot day that is hosting important guests. He is the most important ambassador for the host.

If I had to pick out just one aspect of the many roles of the gamekeeper, I would single out his invaluable contribution to the conservation of the countryside. Of course he does not achieve this entirely on his own, in particular he needs the financial commitment of the estate/farm owner. However the keeper's (and his key helpers) constant attention to predator control combined with his continual planting and husbandry of hedgerows and coverts, and his programme of providing food and water for his game birds ensures the existence of a massive variety of wildlife. Especially the myriad of species of song birds.

Forgetting shooting for a moment, the next time you are in the countryside, look around you. Notice the healthy looking woods, tall thick hedgerows, wide headlands sporting a mass of wild flowers and well-maintained clearly signposted footpaths. Whilst you are looking, just listen and enjoy the variety of bird calls. Having seen and heard these things, you could be certain that you are in, or close to a well-run game shoot.

Chapter Nine
First Driven game Day

Welcome to your first day out on the peg. Today is the day that you put all that theory into practice, but remember that your most important objective is to savour all your new experiences and to enjoy yourself.

Come into the pub and meet your fellow Guns; be reassured they all started JUST like you and will be keen to warmly welcome you. After coffee and introductions, we will all sit down to a hearty cooked breakfast - the only way to start a game day. Do bring your shot gun in with you, where it will be kept in a safe place (guns must never be left in unattended vehicles).

Breakfast

On the days that I organize, I like to start with a sit-down breakfast. Some of the Guns may have been travelling for an hour or two, so will have had an early start and are unlikely to have had a full breakfast before they left home. There may be Guns who know each other well but have not seen each other for a while; so sitting down to a leisurely breakfast and catching up on news, makes for a very nice start to the day.

The most important objective of this style of day start is to give those Guns that have not met before, the chance to sit down together and get to know each other. Bearing in mind that the game day is firstly a social occasion, the more the Guns can relax in each other's company, the better the ambiance; being able to walk to the pegs for the first drive of the day knowing your neighbours' names helps to make everyone feel more comfortable.

Time to depart for the shoot which is quite close by. When we are all parked at the shoot lodge, everyone needs to put all their kit for the day into the Gun bus which we will all be travelling around in. Do make sure that all your kit is put on board, because once we leave for the first drive, we do not return to the lodge until lunch time.

Kit Check

Let us check your kit: Gun in its carrying slip (bag) cartridge bag, full of course, ear defenders, dark shooting glasses just in case we are blessed with a low winter sun, shooting hat, waterproof boots, top coat and waterproof over trousers, spare case of 250 cartridges. Always take far more cartridges than you could possibly use to every shoot that you attend. Firstly, if you are a guest and run out of cartridges, you have implied that you did not expect to get much shooting and therefore had not rated the shoot very highly! Secondly, if you are on a very busy peg 'in the hot seat' and run out of cartridges, you can bet that Sod's Law will prevail, because your neighbouring Guns will be using different calibres. I once ended a drive with one cartridge remaining in one barrel. I was in full view of my host - a very close call!

Now we can go and meet the shoot captain and listen to his brief before he gets you all to draw numbers and explain the numbering system

The Shoot Captain's Brief

The shoot captain's brief will be along these lines:

> *'Good morning Ladies and Gentlemen, welcome to the shoot. Today you will be shooting a mixture of partridges and pheasants. Please feel free to shoot winged vermin (magpies, crows, jays and pigeons) but please do not shoot them until after a game bird has flown through the line.'*

Invariably it is the winged vermin that flies out towards the line of Guns very early on in the drive, particularly if the game birds are going to be flushed from woodland. Being totally wild birds, their survival instincts cause them to take off as soon as beaters appear. At this stage of the drive it is unlikely that all of the beating team are strategically positioned. The game birds soon become educated that the sound of shots constitutes danger, so they walk or fly out on the flanks before the beaters have got them to flushing points where they will fly over the line of Guns. An uneducated, undisciplined, line of Guns can quickly ruin the efforts of the keeper and his team, by blasting away at pigeons in the early stages of a drive -very frustrating!

Back to the brief:

> *'Under no circumstances is anything to be shot on the ground, and continuing on the theme of safety, when birds are flushed from woodland, please ensure that they have sky behind them before you shoot. When you get to your pegs, be ready to shoot - there is no drive start signal but there will be two blasts on a horn to signal the end of the drive. Please do not shoot after the drive end horn. Leave your empty cartridge cases in a neat pile near your peg where a man will come along and pick them up. Please pick up birds that have fallen close to your peg, and if you can manage to carry them back to the* ***game cart*** *(a trailer or open backed pick up that has rails that braces of birds can be hung over to allow air to flow between them; keeping the meat in best condition) that would be very helpful. Please leave birds that have fallen further back to the picking-up team.*
>
> *You may have the odd Woodcock fly through the line, which we would rather you did not shoot. We do also have on the estate, a couple of pure white pheasants, which we definitely do not want you to shoot; in fact we will ask you to make a sizable donation to our pet charity if you do shoot one!'*

Not shooting the white pheasants stems from an era long ago when large shooting estates employed a **head keeper** and a number of **beat-keepers**. These beat-keepers were each responsible for a defined area of the shoot. With their helpers, they fed the birds on their beats by hand. They would be feeding at first light and at dusk, so having a few white birds to show up in poor light conditions gave a visible reassurance that the birds were present. In modern gameshooting the penalty for shooting for white pheasants is merely a humorous way of raising money for worthwhile organisations.

Return to the brief:

> *'We will try to complete five drives today. Four this morning, with a soup break after the first two. Then lunch at about 1 p.m. here in the lodge. There will be one drive after lunch, followed by tea at about 4 p.m. For those of you on a travel time table;you should be free to leave no later than 4.30 p.m.*
>
> *We will now draw for peg numbers, you will be eight Guns, numbering right to left and moving up three. When you are a flank Gun and can see that moving away from the line, may put you under some birds, please feel free to move. Do be very aware of the flank Flag men/beaters.*
>
> *We will always be returning to the Gun bus after each drive, so you only need take sufficient cartridges for one drive to your pegs. Please make sure that all your kit is on the Gun bus. The weather forecast indicates that we should remain dry. Have a very nice day.'*

The Author, John King, (second left, front row) with a team of Guns about to board the Gun bus to head off for the first drive of the day

Guns in their Gun bus' en-route' to the first drive

So we are on our way to the first drive; and I noted that you drew number eight. So you will be the flank Gun on the left hand edge of the line.

We have arrived, so time to disembark - grab your gun and cartridge bag. You are number eight on the end of the line so you are going to walk the furthest from the Gun bus. Two related issues to think about, do you want to carry your bag holding at least 100 cartridges on a long walk to your peg; where, as the flank Gun you are unlikely to have a mass of shooting? Yes you always want to have more cartridges with you than you are likely to use, but your coat pockets will easily hold 50 - just fill your pocket up and leave you bag on the bus.

Before we start walking to your peg, look over to your right where you will see a block of maize that the beaters will be flushing the birds from. If you look to the far end of the maize, you will see the beaters lined out. But where they are now is not where they started from. Behind where they are stood is a block of woodland. Whilst the shoot captain was giving his brief and we were loading up the bus, those beaters were quietly blanking that woodland into the maize (walking slowly in a line through the wood, gently tapping their sticks so that the birds are encouraged to move forward into the maize.)

The beaters will wait quietly in that position until the shoot captain calls the keeper on his radio to tell him that the Guns are lined out on their pegs and are ready. On the near side of the maize you can see three guys with flags stood about 30 yards apart. Those three flag men will walk ahead of the beating line. They are there to discourage the birds from flying out of the maize to the sides. We can't see them, but there will also be **flag men/ flag women** the other side of that maize. If birds do fly to the sides, the flags are shaken in the air making a distinctive sound and very visible movement in an attempt to turn the birds towards the line of Guns. The flags are usually made from pieces of plastic fertilizer sacks tacked to sticks. The bright pieces of plastic are very easily seen and make plenty of noise when they are shaken. You will see that the block of maize ends about 40 yards from that tall hedge; so any birds that have not flushed as the beating line moves forward, will take off as they come to the end of the maize and hopefully fly over the hedge towards the waiting line of Guns

Arriving at the Peg; Safety Checks.

Let us get you to your peg. Well here you are at number eight peg. It is quite normal that each of the other Guns wished you luck as you walked past their pegs. They all want you to do well. Take your gun out of its slip, but do not load yet. Your first task is to look around you and establish all of the potential danger parameters; you can see your immediate neighbour on your right, so you are mentally establishing that invisible halfway line and an angle that will always ensure that your barrels are always safely well above him. Now look to your left and slightly behind you; there are two flag men walking slowly up the hedge line, one of them will eventually be in-line with you and the hedge. There will also be flag men the other side of that hedge. Now turn right around, note that there are two people with their picking-up dogs. They could well move as the drive progresses; so you must continually be aware of their position and the location of those flag men.

Turn back and face the drive and load two cartridges, but do not close the gun yet; there is always a waiting period before the birds start to flush. Look a covey of partridges flying over the middle of the line. Six shots, and I saw one bird fall; now I see another one that has **towered** (a bird that has been hit, flies on quite a long way then suddenly drops dead out of the sky) about 100 yards behind the line; one of the picking-up dogs that you saw behind you, has just retrieved it. That of course is why they are there.

You can close your gun now, barrels up at a safe height. Look to your right! A single partridge. OK, it took you by surprise, your neighbour could have shot it but he was being a gentleman and left it to you. Look left! A covey of partridges; well done! You weren't sure if the shot was safe because of those flag men. Good, you can never be wrong for not shooting.

Just open your gun for a second and take out the cartridges, we will move about 10 yards closer to the hedge and maybe get you a better chance of a shot. There are two partridges coming straight towards you. Hard luck, could have been a right-and-left but they have flown on. Your neighbour has just shot a right-and-

The keeper marshalling his team of beaters through the game crop. He is also acting as a flank flagman

left we must congratulate him when the drive has finished. Pheasants are now flushing over the Guns further down the line. Someone is shooting very well down there; the pickers-up will be busy. This is a typical drive for this type of shoot, the partridges flush first, with the pheasants flying out later in the drive. Hopefully you may get one or two over you before the drive ends.

Here is your chance, a cock pheasant flying to your left. It is a perfectly safe shot well above those flag men. That one got away too! Do not worry, you will get plenty more opportunities today. You shot straight at that bird, I know it looked so big you felt that you could not miss! Remember: Point at the head, then push in front. You have been too busy to notice, but every other Gun in the line has missed at least one bird, and others quite a few. That is perfectly normal. The horn has just sounded, so unload your gun and put it away in the slip. Don't be frustrated that you did not get a bird on your first drive, you did not get much to shoot at as number eight Gun which is to be expected. We moved off your peg so just pick up those empty cartridge cases and put them by the peg where they will be easy to spot.

If you look to your right you can enjoy watching your neighbour working his Labrador. The dog has retrieved one of the partridges from his master's right-and-left and has been sent for the other one. He has got it - pretty to watch isn't it? When your neighbouring Gun shot each of his birds, his dog **marked** them; that is it knew where each bird had fallen, and has remembered where they are.

Pheasants flushed perfectly over a line of Guns

The picking-up dogs back behind that Gun may well have also marked those birds, but their owners have not allowed their dogs to run in and pick up those birds because they know that it is bad form to pick birds that a Gun's dog has marked. The picking-up team that were waiting set well back from the Guns, are now moving forward towards the Gun line working their dogs to pick up fallen birds. The dogs will not have seen many of the birds fall, so they could not have marked them as they were shot; therefore they are finding the birds via their scent rather than sight and memory. Some of these Guns in the middle of the line have collected quite a few birds, so we will help them by carrying some back to the game cart.

Here we are at the game cart; note that the birds are being tied together at the neck in pairs (a brace) so that they can be hung tidily over the cart rails. So back to the Bus and off to the next drive, your fellow Guns seem very happy. As good sportsmen they are congratulating each other on successes, but loudly confessing their own failures. As we approach the next drive you might want to top up your pockets with cartridges, unless you choose to carry your cartridge bag. It is up to you, however I try to carry as little as possible.

Second Drive

Time to disembark again, and a shorter walk this time to peg number three. Here we are at the peg. Note that it is only numbered on one side and that it is leaning at an angle. That gives you, the Gun, two chances to make sure that you stand facing in the correct direction:

1. The Gun always stands on the numbered side of the peg.
2. The peg is angled to point in the direction that the birds will be coming from.

I have seen Guns arrive at their pegs and face in the wrong direction; they must feel quite silly when they look down the line and notice that all the other Guns are facing the other way.

Good, I can see that you are having a good look around to establish all the potential danger parameters. All the Guns are out in the open so your neighbours at two and four are obvious. Look round behind you; there is a wood. You cannot see them this time, but the picking-up team are waiting well back in the wood. During this drive the birds will be flushed from that wood that is about 80 yards in front of you. Look straight ahead to the left hand side of the wood and you will see a man with something quite bright coiled around his shoulder. That is a **sewelling line** (a long piece of rope that will stretch the width of the wood). Every couple of feet along the rope a bright piece of plastic - yes from the same fertilizer bags - has been inserted into the rope. One end of the rope has been tied to a tree or stake about a foot above the ground, the other end of the rope has been walked to the other side of the wood.

We cannot see it from here, but a swathe has been cut through the wood to create a 'flushing ride'. The beaters will be slowly tapping their way forward through the trees; some birds will flush, but many will keep walking forward. When they reach the edge of the flushing area they will see the sewelling line which is now being jerked to startle them enough to cause them to take off. The open area makes it very easy to fly up above the trees then forward over the Guns at a good sporting height. Without the use of the sewelling line and flushing ride, many of the birds would carry on walking right to the edge of the wood and flush out low, all taking off at once.

There are probably a couple of Spaniels with the beaters being worked under control to flush birds out from brambles or extra thick undergrowth. A couple of partridges have just flushed out wide of number one, so I would be ready now. Keep your barrels well above the trees; remember there are beaters in that wood!

Here you go, a classic driven partridge coming over you. Point, shut, lock, step and Push!

I'm afraid you shot to the left of it; in your excitement you forgot to shut your left eye. Don't worry, I am sure that you are in a good spot here. Here comes another one flying to your left, it is your bird. Well done, great shot. Reload, here is another bird to your right, remember lock extra tight. Well done, another one down. Reload.

Look out past number one peg, a partridge flushed out of the wood, followed by a pheasant. See how the partridge starts out in front of the pheasant, but now the

A Labrador retrieving a French partridge

pheasant is overtaking the partridge. The partridge is small with a very quick wing beat, so it looks very fast. The truth is that it cannot fly as fast as the pheasant, which, because it is so much bigger, looks quite slow. This provides one of the main challenges of modern mixed bird game shooting. Here comes a pheasant. Whoops! Head off stock, here comes another one. Good shot. There are more coming towards you, pick your birds take your time. OK some got away, but you got a couple more. Well done, ah there goes the horn. Put your gun away, and let us leave these cartridge cases tidily on the peg.

You have been too busy to notice but your right hand neighbour has not had shooting. The birds that did fly to him were a little low so he let them fly on. His dog however has marked your birds. You could invite your neighbour to let his dog pick up your birds that have fallen close to the edge of the wood, while you pick the two birds that fell very close to you.

Elevenses

You have made a new dog friend, he thinks that you are a 'good egg'. Let us head back to the bus and take these birds to the game cart en route. Put your gun on the bus. We are going to enjoy elevenses: hot soup and sausages (well we have not eaten since breakfast and that was almost three hours ago).

Your fellow Guns are full of praise for your performance on that drive, you better have just a small tot of **sloe gin** (made from the sloe berry from the wild blackthorn bush - a traditional game day tipple), so that you can acknowledge the congratulatory toast.

Whilst we are stopped here socialising, the beaters will probably stop for a quick tea/coffee break; then they will be off to start blanking-in for the next drive. We have all done justice to the soup, sausages and sloe gin, so back on the bus to travel to the next drive, where you will be number six and hopefully in the thick of it. Good! I see you are replenishing your cartridges.

Third Drive

Here we are; this drive will feel different because all the guns will be lined out in this wood. Let us find peg number six - there you go, five yards in front of you. Firstly, make sure you know exactly where your neighbours are, and make sure that they know exactly where you are. Walk over to each of them and let them know that you are totally aware of their positions. Invite your neighbour at number five peg to let his dog pick any birds behind you as he wishes. The ground cover here is very thick, with plenty of brambles. You should spend time now clearing a patch around you peg, pull brambles and bits of branches out of the way; now trample the ground so that your feet have a nice secure platform to move safely on. You do not want to risk tripping over with a loaded gun in your hands. The beaters are working towards us through another wood hoping to flush pheasants across a gap then over the Guns just above these trees. They will be quite testing, as you will not see them for very long.

Guns to your right are already shooting, so you need to be loaded and ready. 'Over number six!' A picker-up behind you saw that pheasant coming towards you. His cry of 'over' is a traditional warning of an approaching bird. Now you know how quick they are going to be. You don't need to be distracted by me now; just shoot at birds you think are yours, safe and sporting. Well you are putting plenty of lead in the air, and have shot three so far. Keep it up.

Can you hear that screeching? That is the alarm call of the jay. I can see two of them flitting between the tress ahead of you. One of them is coming towards you now, have a go when you feel that you have a clear shot. Well sadly your two barrels did not account for it; but number seven gun did bring it down behind you. The jay is a very pretty bird to look at, but definitely a wolf in sheep's clothing - it loves to take other birds eggs, and will take small very young chicks.

There is the horn - gun away and tidy up at the peg first. A lot of empty cases there; how many birds do you think you got? Yes, I agree, I counted five. You were too busy to notice; but when your neighbour accounted for that jay, the picker-up behind you walked forward immediately and picked it up. He did not want to risk any of his dogs trying to pick it. A wounded jay can give a dog a very bad bite with its very sharp beak and could also hang on to a dog's mouth causing great pain and potentially ruining a good picking-up dog. We will walk back towards that picker-up; but you and your neighbours will need to liaise with him about numbers of birds picked up, because number five's dog will have picked some.

The cover here is hard work for the dogs, so we do not want them hunting for birds that have already been picked up.

Fourth Drive

Right, back to the bus and off for the last drive of the morning. Here we are at the fourth drive; I don't think that you will need a mass of cartridges here, a good pocket full should be plenty. Just a short walk to number one peg. There are a couple of additional safety factors to think about at this peg: Firstly, your number two Gun neighbour is now on rising land above you to your left, so you need to be very conscious about the height of anything you shoot at on your left hand side. Secondly there is an unmarked road down below you to your right where, in addition to vehicles, there may also be pedestrians and horse riders. You just need to be very vigilant to your right hand side - there are also two pickers-up the other side of that road hidden by the hedge.

On this drive, partridges and pheasants will be flushed from a block of maize that is out of your vision on higher ground to your left. Two partridges have already flown out a long way to your right, and there go some more. Stay unloaded and we will move off our peg about 30 yards to our right. Now load up; be conscious that as we have moved down hill, we no longer have your left-hand neighbour in view, but we know exactly where he is. Here is a covey of partridges flying to your right. OK you chose not to shoot. Here is a single bird to your right. Still not shooting, because you are nervous about that road. Very good decision; if you stick to that 'if in doubt don't' rule you will always be fine.

There is a great deal of shooting to our left so the birds are flying as intended. Now here is a nice high partridge to your left, well shot! Here is a pheasant on the same flight line. I'm afraid you were behind that with both barrels! Remember point at the pheasant's head and then push in front, don't shoot until you can see a good foot lead. Hopefully you will get another chance. Bad luck, there goes the horn. Put your gun away and we will pick up these cases and walk back to your peg. You had a quiet time there, but that is why we have the numbering systems to try to spread the shooting evenly between the Guns. It is not an exact science, but generally works out pretty well.

Your partridge dropped very close to the game cart, so we don't need to pick that up. However, it sounded like your neighbours had a lot of shooting, so maybe we should go and help them to carry their birds back to the cart. Well the amount of birds seems much smaller than the piles of empty cartridge cases at the pegs - looks like the birds won! Just how it should be.

Lunch

Back to the bus then back to the lodge for lunch. We need to put our clean shoes on to go into the lodge. Someone is staying with the bus to look after the guns and kit, so you can leave everything on board. Let us go in and enjoy socialising with your fellow Guns while you all have a pleasant shoot lunch.

Off to the Last Drive of the Day

Just as we are all feeling warm, cosy, relaxed and lethargic, it is time for action again. Boots and coats on and back on board the Gun bus to travel to the last drive. Here we are, time to disembark - this time bring your cartridge bag with you, you will note that the other Guns have their bags with them.

When there is just one drive after lunch, it tends to be quite a long one with (hopefully) a good number of high sporting birds being presented over the line of Guns. This is achieved by a great deal of physical effort and careful strategic planning by the game keeper and his team.

Whilst we were lingering over our cheese, biscuits and coffee, the beating team were already hard at work gently tapping through a large expanse of woodland. They had probably been working for at least 30 minutes before we arrived. They have now split strategically into three groups; two walking in slowly from each flank and one coming in slowly from the far side of the cover towards the Gun line. This is predominately a pheasant drive with birds being flushed from a mixture of woodland and maize cover crops. During the 'blanking-in' of this drive and possibly during earlier ones, **stops** may have been put in place. These are members of the beating team strategically placed, typically at the start of hedges and ditches. They tap their sticks continually throughout the blanking-in process to discourage the birds from walking quietly away from the drive location.

You probably have not noticed, but you have not heard any voices from the beating line, only the sound of tapping sticks and shaken plastic flags. Maybe, if you were close enough to the keeper or key person, you may have heard quiet voices on the radio. Loud voices carry the sound long distances, and may well startle the birds to take off out of the drive area. The best shoots always have an aura of quiet efficiency.

The birds are going to appear from the top of that bank in front of you, and you have already decided that your gun ready position will always have your barrels above the trees at the top of that bank. Your neighbours are in clear view, but during this drive you will have two back Guns. You are number four peg, and if you turn around you will see one of them is about 30 yards behind you and the other is behind numbers six and seven pegs.

Having 'back' Guns on a drive like this is quite typical, because some of the flushes of birds will be more than a single line of Guns can cope with. There is an air of nervous anticipation now, as all the Guns are expecting this drive to be busy and testing. Here comes the first flush - high aren't they? Many bangs, much cordite, but nothing down out of that flush. It generally takes a few shots to get to full alertness after lunch.

Remember 'timing and lock' that you practised during your high bird practice sessions. Here comes another flush. Pick the bird nearest to you and point at its head, mount the gun slowly, lock extra tight and push hard in front. Reload and try to lock tighter for you next bird. Never mind! Here is one just over your left shoulder, now step round shoot to miss it a yard in front. Well done! Your first really high pheasant. You will have plenty more over you , take your time and pick out your birds. Best I just let you get on with it now. What a spectacular drive to finish on, and I am sure that you will remember those high birds that you brought down for a long time to come. Just look at your pile of empty cartridge cases - no! I wouldn't bother to count them, just remember what a great time that you had.

Here come the beaters on their way back to their wagon; let us wait here and thank them for their hard work during the day. It is good for them to know that the Guns appreciate their efforts and skills. We will help pick up some birds before the bus takes us back to the lodge. Time to disembark, unload the bus, clean the guns and take off our boots and outer clothing. We can enjoy a nice cup of tea and slice of cake in the lodge whilst the shoot captain waits for the keeper. Here is the keeper; he is telling the shoot captain what the total bag is for the day (the total number of birds shot in their individual species).

Pheasant flushing over tall trees, then climbing higher over the line of Guns

In a few minutes the shoot captain will give each of you Guns a **shoot card** (the card will list the names of today's Guns and the details of the bag). Some of the Guns will keep a game book in which they will religiously enter the details from the shoot card for every day that they attend, so that they have a complete record of all their game shooting. There are game books in families that have been handed down through the generations, some of which make for fascinating reading. You may decide to start your own game book.

.... Date ....

Pheasants	**GUNS**
Woodcock	....
Partridges	....
Duck	....
Hares	....
Rabbits	....
Various	....
	....
TOTAL	....
	....

A typical game card, ready to record the details of the day.

A typical game book

Inside a typical game book

When you have thanked the shoot captain, you have one further traditional ritual before you say goodbye to your fellow Guns. It is now time to tip the game keeper who will give you a brace of birds as you do so. As this is your first time, let me advise you that your tip is offered discreetly. The easiest way is to fold up the money into the palm of your right hand, as you approach him he will offer you a brace of birds with his left hand. You accept the birds with your left hand and shake hands normally as you say thanks for your day.

On this shoot, you will be given oven ready birds, which more and more shoots are doing so that Guns can offer them to their friends to encourage more people to enjoy eating game. Guns may also take extra oven ready birds by arrangement.

So there ends your first formal driven day. I do hope that you enjoy many more.

Chapter Ten
Simple & Delicious Game Recipes

Pheasant Leg Confit

Confit is a French method of preserving meat, traditionally duck, in fat. It is a method particularly well suited to pheasant legs as, although very tasty, they can be a little dry. This is a very useful recipe for those people who love pheasant breast, but never know what to do with the legs as the confit will keep in the fridge for at least a month.

Serves 4-6

6 pheasant legs
200g coarse sea salt
2 bay leaves
a couple of garlic cloves crushed
a sprig of thyme
a slug of brandy
800g duck fat

The first stage of the confit is to cure the meat. Rub the salt into the pheasant legs then place them into a container just large enough to contain the pheasant legs, salt, bay leaves, garlic, thyme and brandy. Do not worry if you have to pack them in tightly. Cover and leave in the fridge for up to 12 hours.

After you have cured the legs, you will need to rub off the marinade. Do not wash it off. Melt the duck fat with a few more crushed cloves of garlic in a heavy casserole large enough to allow you to submerge the pheasant legs in the now liquid duck fat.

Place in casserole in an oven preheated to 130ºC for 3-4 hours. The legs are done when the meat is ready to fall easily away from the bones. Take the dish out of the oven and allow it to cool.

Once it is cool, place the legs in an air tight jar, such as a glass Kilner jar, cover in the fat and seal. Keep in the fridge for up to a month.

When you are ready to use the confit remove the legs from their jar, scrape as much of the fat off as possible, and roast in a preheated oven at 180ºC for 20-30 minutes until the skin is crispy. Serve with some quickly steamed savoy cabbage.

Pheasant and Partridge Pie

This is one of my most useful recipes. I have often been called in by people to spend the day cooking up all the game they have collected, and frozen, throughout the season. Portioning it up into servings for 4's, 6's and 8's then freezing it ready to be easily defrosted and made into a yummy game pie.

Serves 4

2 pheasants and 2 partridges (and any other game you have)

for the marinade:

250 ml red wine
2 bay leaves
1 sprig thyme
whole garlic bulb crushed
a glug of olive oil
sea salt and freshly ground pepper
1 celery stalk, ½ leek & 1 carrot

for the pie mix:

a knob of butter
1 tablespoon of olive oil
1 onion (roughly chopped)
1 garlic clove
2 carrots (diced)
2 celery stalks
1 leek
1 tablespoon plain flour
100 ml red wine
400 ml chicken stock
short crust pastry
200 g plain flour
100 g butter diced
a few tablespoons of cold water

Begin by taking the legs and breasts off your birds and dice the breasts. You can take the meat off the legs once they are cooked. Place the meat in a dish with the marinating ingredients, make sure it is well coated. You may have to give it a turn every so often. Leave in the marinade for 24 hours.

The next day, wipe the marinade off the birds (keep the marinade but strain out the herbs and garlic) and brown the meat in a little butter and olive oil in a heavy casserole, you may have to do this in batches.

When you have browned the meat leave it on a plate. In the same casserole, use the oily juices to sweat the onion and garlic. After a couple of minutes add the carrots, leek and celery. Cook for another couple of minutes then return the meat back to the pan and sprinkle over the flour salt and pepper. Cook for a few minutes then add the red wine and marinade. Let this boil for a minute or two then add the stock. Bring to the boil again, give it all a stir, turn off the heat and put the lid on to your casserole. Cook in a preheated oven 180ºC for 1½-2 hours. Check half-way through the cooking time and add more stock if you think it needs it.

Allow to cool and take the meat off the legs and shred back into the mix. Either, place in freezer bags and freeze for later use, or, if you cannot wait, make your pie straight away!

To make pastry, blitz the flour and butter in a food processor until they resemble bread crumbs. Then, on pulse, add the water a tablespoon at a time until the pastry forms a ball. allow to rest in the fridge for 20 minutes before you use. Place the defrosted game mix onto a pie plate or dish and cover in short crust pastry making sure you leave a couple of steam holes. Cook for 30-40 minutes on 180ºC.

Country Game Pâté

This is a rustic, well flavoured pâté; ideal with thick slices of wholemeal bread.

Serves 6-8

350g mixed game bird meat pheasant partridge or pigeon, minced.
450g belly pork, minced
200g pigs liver minced
200 g bacon chopped
1 teaspoon of sea salt (I like Maldon sea salt flakes)
¼ teaspoon mace
1 garlic clove crushed
15 peppercorns and 15 juniper berries crushed in a pestle and mortar
25ml brandy, sherry or port
you will need a 1 kg or 2lb loaf tin (approx.19x12x9cm) or terrine dish
20g streaky bacon to line your tin

Start by placing all your meats and bacon in a bowl. Add all the other ingredients to the meat and mix thoroughly, you will probably have to use your hands to mix really well. Cover and put in the fridge overnight to let all the flavours meld together.

The next day put your oven on 150°C. Line your loaf tin with streaky bacon. Pack your pate mixture into the tin, fold over any loose bits of bacon and cover with tin foil and bake in a roasting tin half-filled with hot water for 1 ½ hours.

When cooked, the pâté will have shrunk quite a lot. Remove from the oven and allow to cool. When it is cool place some weights on it for a few hours, a couple tins of tomatoes are ideal. This will press it and stop it being too crumbly. Turn out the pâté and enjoy in thick slices with crusty bread.

Pot Roasted Pheasant

This is a real family favourite in our house and very simple to make.

Serves 4

2 whole pheasants
a couple of knobs of butter
1 swede roughly diced
2 carrots (roughly chopped)
1 onion (roughly chopped)
2 parsnips (roughly chopped)
2 small turnips (diced)
2 garlic cloves (crushed)
4 rashers streaky bacon
1 tablespoon plain flour
a couple of slices of fresh orange peel and the juice of the orange
200ml red wine
250ml chicken or vegetable stock

Preheat the oven to 180°C

Firstly, melt the butter in a heavy bottomed deep casserole. Once it is sizzling, place your whole seasoned pheasants breast down. Brown and crisp the birds all over then remove them and place on a plate.

Add your chopped onion, swede, parsnip, carrot, turnip, crushed garlic cloves and chopped streaky bacon to the pan with all the birds juices and coat everything and allow to sweat for 5-10 minutes. Add the tablespoon of flour to the vegetables and mix. Next add your red wine. Stir while it heats up again, letting it bubble for a few minutes to burn off some of the alcohol. Then pour in your stock, orange juice and peel. Again bring this to the boil for a few minutes then turn right down to a simmer. Now place your birds back into the pan with the vegetables, giving them a little push down into the liquid, but not covering them completely.

Place a lid on top and cook in the oven for 1 ½ hours at 180ºC.

Half way through the cooking time, take it out and check there are enough juices - add more stock if you think it needs it.

Once this is cooked you need to cut the birds in half. I find a pair of kitchen scissors soon gets this job done. Serve half a bird each with all the delicious vegetables and gravy. I don’t feel the need for any other accompaniments, but if you prefer, try some mashed potato to soak up the gravy.

Roast Partridge with Savoy Cabbage, Bacon and Port

Serves 4

4 partridges
salt and pepper
a few sprigs of thyme
12 slices of streaky bacon
a good knob of butter
olive oil
1 large onion finely chopped
4 cloves of garlic
1 savoy cabbage
150ml chicken stock
150ml tawny port
150g lardons (cubes of bacon or pancetta)

Preheat oven to 200ºC

Start by preparing the birds. Take off the legs, then place a knob of butter and thyme into the cavity of each bird. Season with salt and pepper and wrap each bird with the streaky bacon. Heat some oil and butter In a heavy pan and then sear the birds until the bacon has a golden colour. Place on a plate to one side.

In the same pan, fry the onions and lardons, then the crushed garlic and sliced cabbage. Turn them over in the pan juices add the tawny port and allow to reduce for a couple of minutes then pour the stock over, place the birds on top and roast for 10 minutes.

When the cooking time is up, take it out of the oven and place the birds to one side to rest. Place your pan on a high heat and reduce the cooking sauces for a minute. Give each of your guests a pile of cabbage with a bird on top and some cooking juices poured over the top.

Little Game Pies

These are similar to a pork pie you might put in your picnic, made with a hot water crust pastry. You will need a muffin tin with 12 holes.

for 8 pies:
for the filling
300g of country game terrine mix

for hot water crust pastry
450g plain flour
100g butter
100g lard
180ml water
pinch of salt and pepper

To make the pastry, place the flour salt and pepper in a roomy mixing bowl. Next melt the butter and lard and water in a pan and then allow it to boil for a few moments. Pour the liquid into the flour and stir vigorously until it starts to form a dough. Lift it out onto a floured surface and knead until it is smooth. Wrap in cling film and rest in the fridge for half an hour.

Preheat the oven to 200ºc.

Take 2/3 of the pastry and make 8 equally sized balls then roll in to circles bigger than the hole in the tin. Push the pastry down into the tin leave an edge proud of the tin. Next, place your pate mix into the cases. Fill them so they are have a slight mound and use the rest of the pastry to make the lids. Brush the edges with egg before you place your lids on top and squeeze the edges to seal. Cut a hole in the top to allow the steam to escape, brush with egg and cook for 30-35 minutes until the pastry is golden brown. Allow to cool and enjoy.

Note From the Author

John King is very pleased to record here, that he has been able to enjoy Jo's excellent cooking and delightful varied menus on many occasions.

If you would like to treat your family, friends and special guests to one of Jo's delicious game dishes or any other of her culinary delights at your dinner party/ important event, you can contact her via John at; admin@johnkingcoaching.com

Closing Thoughts

My most important thought at this point is 'have I managed to achieve my objectives?' Throughout the preceding pages, I have been trying to present a structured format which mirrors the process that I have taken so many newcomers to game shooting through. If any of you who have been thinking of taking up game shooting have been encouraged to take that step, then I am, of course, delighted.

For those of you that are fairly novice game shots, I really do hope that I have answered the questions, that perhaps you were not sure who, or how, to ask. I also hope that I have described a system of shooting that you have found easy to follow, and that you have been motivated to practice.

Those of you that are already very experienced game shots hopefully have found some hints, tips and snippets of information that are useful to you. If you feel that the information that I have provided within this book helps you train and bring on other newcomers to game shooting, I will be especially pleased.

It occurs to me that newcomers may well say, 'OK you have whetted my appetite, but how do I go about starting and finding our game shooting?' At risk of stating some avenues that may be obvious; here are some simple suggestions:

Finding Suitable Game Shooting

The most logical starting place is with your friends. Speak to people that you know are involved in game shooting, and tell them you're interested in taking it up. These people should be those whose words you feel you can trust, and whose company you would enjoy.

Your local shooting school that provides game shooting lessons, may well also organize game days. Local syndicates may also be asking the school to introduce suitable candidates to fill their vacancies.

Note: Good syndicates rarely advertise vacancies, so do take every opportunity to spread the word wherever you can about your keenness to join a good syndicate.

Take up the best quality field shooting magazines. They all list available game shooting in their classified pages. You will also find the best sporting agents listed there, most of whom will be offering vacancies in their roving syndicates.

A very good route to finding shooting that suits your requirements is via www.gunsonpegs.com. This is an excellent website put together by people who really understand shooting and it is completely free to use! They have a very good relationship with their members offering shooting, and the system is designed for shoots to be able to easily upload their availability and for the Guns to then find what they are looking for. You simply register on the website and they will then put you in direct contact with the shoots that you are interested in.

It may well be that you are curious about, and keen to try out becoming a beater. In that case if you do not have personal contacts; go to www.basc.org.uk. The British Association For Shooting And Conservation. They will be able to put you in touch with local keepers via their game keepers organization.

Some of you may be very keen to be able to witness a complete game day, to see exactly what goes on; which is an approach that I would encourage every potential newcomer to take.

Do ask your game shooting contacts, including your local shooting school, to help you to arrange to be part of a full game day as a spectator, but included in all the social aspects of the day.

If you do not have any suitable contacts, please contact me via email at: admin@johnkingcoaching.com and I will make every effort to get you along on one of the game days that I organise for my clients who would be very welcoming towards you. Please accept though, that there is only limited availability.

My concluding hope is that I have been able to offer information which has enhanced your understanding of game shooting, enabled you to improve your own shooting skills and helped you to maximise your enjoyment of game shooting.

About The Author

John considers himself a late starter, as he did not discover how deadly he could be with his .177 BSA Air rifle on his families' smallholding in Warwickshire until he was 8 years old.

He found the starlings in the Ash tree at the piggery worthy targets and gave them his marksman's attention whenever he could. With his terrier, Ginny, he waged war on the rats in the chicken runs; they usually considered themselves the winners.

Alongside his country boy peers; he graduated to pigeons and rabbits in addition to water rats and moorhens along canals, rivers and streams. When air gun pellets were in short supply, the hunting weaponry was supplemented with catapults plus bows and arrows (all homemade of course).

Like all the other village boys, he could be found in the beating line on the local farm shoot enviously eyeing up the shotguns of the adult Guns.

At the ripe old age of 10 years he bagged his first quarry with a shotgun - a squirrel and a mallard - using a borrowed 16 bore *side-by-side* (all this without his non-shooting families' knowledge)! This young black sheep had already found his favourite pursuits, which he indulged in whenever he could escape school and chores.

Joining the Royal Navy at 15 years old brought his field sports to an abrupt end. However, John was never far from handling or being involved in something that went 'Bang' or 'Boom'. Much of John's 25 years in the RN were spent as a trainer of a variety of weaponry, including demolitions - very big bangs that made him very happy!

He arrived at the Royal Navy Leadership School in the wilds of Wiltshire, as a trainer during the early 1970s. Within days, he had discovered shotguns and cartridges in the armoury which, to his joy, he was invited to use as he wished. Very soon rabbits, partridges and pheasants ("poached" which probably is not describing the way that they were cooked) were finding their way to the chef's galley.

Hearing of the shot gunning expertise of the new arrival, the Commanding Officer sent for John and told him that there was a clay pigeon trap on the Sports field and that "Chief Petty Officer King was to become the new clay shooting instructor for the students attending the leadership courses." John, of course, replied "Aye Aye Sir" and took up his new extra-curricular role with immediate effect.

He did not let on that he had never seen a clay pigeon and did not know anything about clay pigeon shooting.

He did however recognise what great fun clay shooting was and, at the earliest opportunity, enrolled himself on a CPSA Coaches course. Two years later, he qualified as a CPSA Senior Sporting Coach.

John's new life in Wiltshire also allowed him to re-immerse himself in the farming community and enjoy his field sports at every opportunity. After leaving the Leadership School, John was sent to Southampton University.

As an RN Warrant officer, he found himself studying psychology as a full time student; two years later, he was posted to Portland in Dorset to take up a new role. Whilst serving there he built the Royal Navy's first ever Sporting Clay shooting layout, and was instrumental in getting Clay Shooting established as a 'recognised' Naval sport.

When John left the navy during 1987 he set up the now renowned Barbury Shooting School with his wife Maureen near their home in Wiltshire (they sold the school in 2007, although John happily remains there as a much sought after coach). He soon built up an enviable reputation for his unique style of coaching and became very much involved in the game shooting community. His close involvement with many game shooting families (he now confesses to coaching three generations in some families) has enabled him to gain access to their very exclusive private game shoots, where he was invited to take teams of Guns made up from his game shooting pupil client list (some of whom are still enjoying shooting with him on these private shoots).

He has taken his coaching skills across to the USA a couple of times, and has introduced his clients there (many of whom still return on a regular basis) to British game shooting. Countless other nationalities of clients have been coached to great game shooting success by him.

John is just as enthusiastic about coaching as he ever was. He has no plans to retire; continues to run his highly popular days on private estates, and is looking forward to introducing many more pupils to successful game shooting:

www.johnkingcoaching.com

admin@johnkingcoaching.com

Swindon, Wiltshire, UK